PENGUIN BUSINESS

THE MONK IN THE CORNER OFFICE

Gopi Krishnaswamy is a former senior executive-turned-Zen practitioner and mindfulness teacher. Previously a managing director at the iconic Silicon Valley design firm IDEO, he has gone beyond the boardroom to study under various Zen masters, including living at Master Thich Nhat Hanh's monastery in Thailand.

Today, he works at the intersection of mindfulness, emotional intelligence and leadership, with a focus on practical, accessible tools for daily life.

As founder of Llama, he helps companies build cultures where well-being and high performance go hand in hand. He has trained leaders across five continents, reaching over 1,00,000 people from organizations such as Deloitte, the Boston Consulting Group, the Aditya Birla Group, etc., and has spoken at global forums including Nasscom as well as the governments of the UK, Germany and Canada. Gopi also teaches Search Inside Yourself—the very popular mindfulness-based emotional intelligence programme born at Google.

Gopi's mission is simple yet radical: to demystify meditation and make workplace well-being the norm. His previous book, *Creativity Unleashed: 48 Days to Unlock Your Creative Spirit*, offers a mindfulness-based DIY approach to creativity.

To learn more, or invite him to speak or train on mindfulness and EI, visit www.gopikrishnaswamy.com.

The MONK in the CORNER OFFICE

WORK LIFE WISDOM FOR THE 21st CENTURY

GOPI KRISHNASWAMY

PENGUIN BUSINESS

An imprint of Penguin Random House

PENGUIN BUSINESS

Penguin Business is an imprint of the Penguin Random House group of companies whose addresses can be found at global.penguinrandomhouse.com

Published by Penguin Random House India Pvt. Ltd
4th Floor, Capital Tower 1, MG Road,
Gurugram 122 002, Haryana, India

First published in Penguin Business by Penguin Random House India 2025

Copyright © Gopi Krishnaswamy 2025

Illustrations by Kalyani Mehendale

All rights reserved

10 9 8 7 6 5 4 3 2 1

The views and opinions expressed in this book are the author's own and the facts are as reported by him which have been verified to the extent possible, and the publishers are not in any way liable for the same.

Please note that no part of this book may be used or reproduced in any manner for the purpose of training artificial intelligence technologies or systems.

ISBN 9780143475521

Typeset in Adobe Garamond Pro by MAP Systems, Bengaluru, India
Printed at Thomson Press India Ltd, New Delhi

This book is sold subject to the condition that it shall not, by way of trade or otherwise, be lent, resold, hired out or otherwise circulated without the publisher's prior consent in any form of binding or cover other than that in which it is published and without a similar condition including this condition being imposed on the subsequent purchaser.

www.penguin.co.in

Contents

A Note to the Reader   vii

Part 1: Mastering Your Self
Day 0: The Journey Begins   3
Day 1: An Adventure Called Uncertainty   8
Day 2: Who Am I?: A Journey of Self-Awareness   24
Day 3: Meeting the Ghosts of Self-Criticism   48
Day 4: Emotions and the Human Condition   74

Part 2: Leading Yourself: Building an Intentional Life
Day 5: Mindfulness: A Way of Life   109
Day 6: Values, Motivation and Manifesting a Life of Meaning   144
Day 7: Bend, Not Break: A Fluid Quality of Resilience   164

Part 3: Leading Others and Bringing Out the Best in Them
Day 8: Empathy and Building Great Teams   193

Day 9: Compassionate Leadership 224
Day 10: Purpose and Transformation 242
Day 11: Another Journey Begins 288

Acknowledgements 295

A Note to the Reader

As we navigate a volatile and complex world where AI is competing with and even replacing humans, emotional intelligence or EI has become more important than IQ. How could one develop this kind of intelligence and the skills that make up EI? Through training programmes? Books? Perhaps there is no single answer.

However, there is one skill that helps—mindfulness. It is arguably the mother of all skills. Both EI and mindfulness are vast topics and have already been explored by many exceptional minds. My attempt though is to draw a connection between the two subjects in a simple yet powerful and engaging way that readers can relate to.

The Monk in the Corner Office has evolved through decades of my own meditation practices and years of teaching mindfulness and training people in emotional intelligence. Through the characters of Krish and Sid, I've tried to bring to life the timeless wisdom of mindfulness and connect it to the important skills that constitute emotional intelligence. Because time and again, I've seen that mindfulness helps build the skills that are so critical for success at work and life in the 21st century.

Key insights are highlighted through the book for your easy reference and recall. Sid's journal at the end of each chapter is a portal through which you can easily access the important points of each topic and also spark your own reflections.

My suggestion is that you not only read the book as you would a novel—each chapter in sequence—but also go back to the different chapters. Read them again, make notes and reflect on how that particular topic and skill applies to your life.

Having a separate journal would be an excellent way to further reinforce the learning. And finally, as the old saying goes, 'When you teach one person, two people learn!'. So, find a way to share your experience. It is a powerful way to turbocharge your learning.

And above all, enjoy the ride!

Part 1

Mastering Your Self

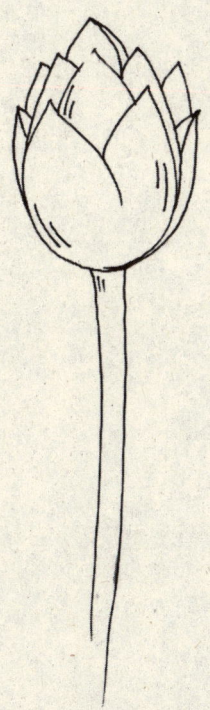

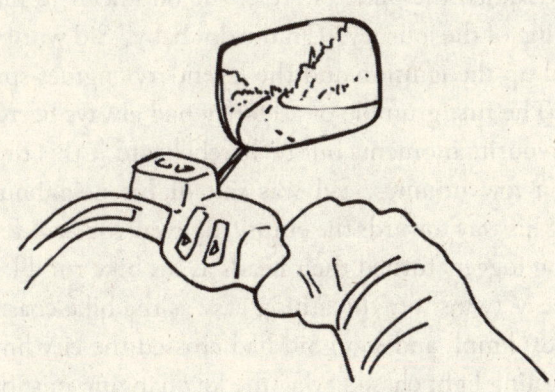

Day 0: The Journey Begins

As he tightened the straps on the saddlebags, Sidharth looked down at the powerful V twin cylinders of his Harley Davidson. As his gaze moved along the dusty Screaming Eagle chrome pipes, a weary unshaven face looked back at him. Dull eyes met briefly and Sid quickly looked away. He was not ready to confront his thoughts. Yet.

He got up and inspected the bike. It was a fine piece, and in the years he had had it, it had earned him many admiring and envious looks.

The city was still quiet, except for the birds sensing the break of dawn. Summer was almost over and the early rains had cooled the city considerably in the last few days.

It was 5 a.m. Sid deeply inhaled the smell of wet earth as he straddled the bike. He reset the odometer to mark the beginning of the journey. 'On the dot baby,' Sid whispered as he fired up the ignition and the legendary engines sputtered to life. The first grumble of a Harley had always been one of Sid's favourite moments but he barely heard it this time.

In a few minutes, Sid was out of his neighbourhood, making his way towards the empty highway roads. A few early morning joggers turned their heads as his bike rumbled past.

The V twins were breathing easy as the bike coasted at a steady 80 kmph and soon Sid had crossed the city limits. As the morning light chased away the low hanging mist over the fields, Sid's mind kept going back to the last few months.

It was one of those things about biking that Sid liked. A good road and a good bike let his mind wander freely. These days, it was mostly in the past. He let the wind tug at the memories that surfaced as he leaned into corners with the same ease as the birds that soared overhead rode the air currents. The road whizzed past just a few inches from his feet, a blurred reminder of reality. He looked back at how it all started.

In the beginning, he had barely even noticed it. He would wake up feeling tired and put it down to the previous night's party. As a rising star at one of the world's leading IT consulting firms, Sid attended several office parties. But last year, especially, he had steadily grown to dislike more and more the polite chatter that these gatherings all started with and the platforms for self-glorification that they invariably ended up as.

That was when the drinks had started helping. A few quick ones in the first hour would dull the pain of having to smile politely at all the faces around him. The next few would allow him to provide socially acceptable comments and finally, the last few would reduce everything around into a bearable blur. The alcohol put him into a restless stupor that later passed for sleep. A sleep during which he often dreamt that he was the clown as the world passed by pointing and smirking at him. The days had been full of caffeine and nicotine. Each day had to keep pace with the restlessness of the night. Or was it the other way round? Sid wasn't sure.

The wind roared, tugging at Sid's jacket as if its sole purpose was ripping it apart but he barely noticed. The engine's steady drone was like a pulse as he effortlessly leaned into another corner. In these moments, the bike felt like an extension of his body as it gracefully bent along with him. Sid was completely in tune with the machine and it felt like time itself was taking a pause. Sid wondered if he had ever been this much in sync with anything in his life. The answer rose from the depths of his mind as if the wind had finally managed to get a grip on it. No!

It had not always been like this. For many years, Sid had been a star. Whether it was in college, or after that, he had always been known as a winner. One who had what it took to be the best and stay at the top. His career had started off on the fast track. The salary and bonuses got better each year. There were several failed relationships, but he had written off each as a testimony to his unwavering dedication to his career.

The last twelve months had become a bit of a blur, though. Caffeine-induced meetings, alcohol-induced sleep and countless miles on flights. And then finally, that fateful morning two weeks ago. The morning he had woken up but collapsed after getting out of bed and taking a few steps towards the bathroom.

The bike slowed suddenly. Involuntarily, his foot had tapped the rear brake as the memory gripped him. Fortunately, the Harley was on a dry road and a quick tap of the front brake ensured the bike did not fishtail. Sid shook his head. Whether it was to reprimand himself for the braking lapse or a shudder resulting from the recollection of that morning, he was not very sure.

The sun was still rising behind him as Sid rolled steadily towards the hills. He could see some windmills in the distance and smiled. He had always liked windmills. They always reminded him of Don Quixote. But this time, it was different. It almost felt like he was a modern version of Don Quixote, charging on his gleaming steed towards the huge arms that sprouted from the hills and stabbed the sky with steely fingers, writhing in anticipation of crushing him.

Sid's mind went back two weeks to that eventful day. The doctors had not been kind. They had been thorough in their diagnosis and ruthless in their communication. In simple non-medical terms, he was burnt out. The writing on the wall was in bright neon letters: STOP.

For a few days, Sid had stayed at the hospital. And while he was there, it dawned on him that he had not taken a break in years. The realization had jarred at first and he had not slept that night. 'What am I doing in life?' he had wondered, as he lay in bed, counting off the hours to daybreak. And as morning approached, in that strange state between sleep and wakefulness, Sid had taken a decision. He would take that break.

It was almost as if the decision itself was an elixir. Sid had got up with a smile, something he had not done in a long time. The next few days had been spent in cementing his decision and informing people. He had sent out a few emails informing his colleagues. Surprisingly, the world had not fallen apart as he had greatly feared. Maybe he was not as indispensable as he had assumed.

For over a year now, Sid had thought about a motorcycle road trip but had never found the courage to just take off. But now, nothing was going to hold him back.

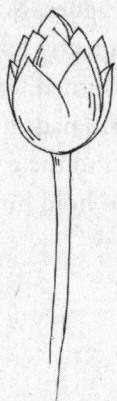

Day 1: An Adventure Called Uncertainty

The truck in front of him belched diesel fumes. He had now been driving for hours and had the company of a truck every few hundred metres on the road. This one was painted in bright colours and had the ubiquitous 'Horn OK Please' phrase written on the back. Over the years, Sid had come across a few different stories about this.

One version Sid had heard was that that this was a custom from the Second World War. Facing a petrol shortage, trucks were often driven on kerosene and kerosene, being more volatile, was prone to exploding at the slightest accident.

And so, to warn drivers behind them, these trucks had 'Horn Please. On Kerosene' painted behind them. Post war, this had morphed into 'Horn Please OK' or 'Horn OK Please'.

There was another version with a marketing spin that Sid liked better. Somewhere in the 60's, the Indian business conglomerate Tatas started marketing a detergent called OK, which had the logo of a lotus flower. The story goes that the Tatas used the trucks they made to market their detergent by painting the backs of the trucks with the lotus symbol and OK. Over time, the logo merged with the 'Horn Please' and today you could see that trucks had 'Horn OK Please' or even 'Horn OK TATA Please' on the back.

As he held back behind the truck, Sid realized the road had a lot of potholes on the right. He slowly moved to the left to avoid the bad patches and make himself visible in the left rear mirror of the truck. He was also looking out for the ubiquitous 'cleaner', the chap who would be hanging out of the left window of the truck.

'Cleaner' was a misnomer. The trucks were almost always dirty.

The cleaner was more of a manual indicator, assistant, whipping boy and wannabe driver all rolled into one who would one day drive his own truck and have his own cleaner.

A hand emerged from the window of the truck and motioned Sid to go ahead. He flipped a gear and the Harley willingly complied.

The barren countryside was giving way to green now with paddy fields stretching out on both sides of the highway. The air felt fresher and the trees swayed gently in the breeze. Bursts of wildflowers by the side of the road added colour to the landscape.

I'll stay on the road for the next hour or so, Sid thought as he stopped briefly for a few sips of water. Roads could be fun if you were in the right mood for them. But they could also be painful, tiring and slow. It was often about perspective. Just like the bottle of water he put back into his rucksack. *Was it half empty? Or half full?* His mind considered the possibilities. *It's always full*, he decided. *Just that one half was full of water and the other half was full of air.*

Growing up, Sid had shown a natural talent for thinking out of the box. He often thought it was this ability that had helped him stay ahead in life. But sometimes he felt it was the same ability that made him imagine problems where there were none.

A big sign on the road informed Sid of a border check post ahead. As he started slowing down, he noticed a line of cars, buses and trucks. On nearing the post, he could see what seemed like a bit of a commotion. 'What is the problem, sir?' Sid asked one of the policemen patrolling the road near where he had stopped. 'Cross-border vehicular movement has been stopped due to some political tension in the neighbouring state, sir,' the constable replied.

'I have ridden a long way and I cannot go back. Can I please go ahead?' Sid pleaded.

'Sorry, sir. Our orders have come from the government and we cannot permit anyone beyond this point. There are many others here like you and they will all start demanding the same thing, sir,' the cop was polite but firm as he stood in the middle of the road with one hand on his rifle.

Sid wheeled the Harley off to the side of the road, parked and sat down on the kerb. He looked up at the sky and saw clouds that threatened rain. Where would he stay? How long would this take?

It was about ten minutes later that he noticed him, a tall man with long, thick silver hair speaking with the same policeman. From their body language, Sid could make out that it was an amicable conversation. In fact, the policeman was being very respectful towards the other man. *Must be some politician or bureaucrat*, he thought as he went back to occupying himself with the challenge he faced. That's when Sid saw the policeman point to him and say something to the man. Then the man started to walk towards him.

As he came closer, Sid could see that he was extremely fit. His faded and frayed blue jeans paired with a thin, loose white shirt revealed a well-toned body. It was hard to tell his age from his face; there was something almost boyish about him.

'Hello!' he called out cheerily as he approached Sid. 'Sit. Sit,' he continued just as Sid involuntarily started to get up. Something about this man commanded respect and Sid had a feeling that he might be a politician or a bureaucrat. 'Hello,' Sid heard himself respond as his mind raced to box this stranger into some familiar category.

'I hear that you are stuck! My friend, the policeman, was just telling me that you have ridden a long way on your big motorcycle. Even from where I was speaking with him, I could make out it was a Harley,' he said pointing to the bike as he plopped himself easily onto the kerbside next to Sid. The man's voice had a certain depth to it. It was a voice that effortlessly commanded attention. Not because it was loud, but because it made you want to hear it again. His eyes were piercing and when he looked at Sid, he made him feel like someone was looking deep into his soul. Sid could still not place his age. His face had a youthful quality that belied the silver hair.

'Yes. I am a bit stuck. I'm almost a whole day's drive away from home. Can't go forward, can't head back either,' Sid said.

The man laughed. 'You have in that sentence summed up what many people can say about their life itself. Stuck!' he said.

Sid was instinctively beginning to like this man. 'I'm Sidharth,' he said as he put his hand out for a handshake. 'Hello Sidharth,' the stranger said as he shook Sid's outstretched hand. The firmness of the handshake was noticeable.

'I'm Krish. I live close by on a farm. I understand you can't ride back right now, especially with the prospect of heavy rain also looming large. You are welcome to come by and rest till you figure out what you can do next.'

Under most circumstances, Sid would not have thought much about this offer before refusing it. Not this time, though. There was something instinctively trustworthy about the man. Moreover, he didn't have too many other options.

'Thank you, sir. That's very kind of you. I would like to do that,' he heard himself say to his own surprise. It was almost as though his gut had made the decision and he was relaying it quickly before anything got in the way.

'Come on then. Let me turn my truck around and you can follow me,' said Krish as he stood up, dusted the back of his jeans and started walking towards a line of cars that were parked to the side of the road.

Sid had always considered himself to be a relatively logical and rational person and yet, here he was, accepting a stranger's offer to shelter him within barely a few minutes of meeting him. *How funny*, Sid thought to himself as he sat astride the motorcycle and heard the comforting roar of the engines coming to life again.

A dusty pick-up backed up from the end of the long line of vehicles and turned around. Sid saw Krish waving to him.

As he started following Krish to his farm, he noticed a crate of vegetables at the back of the pick-up truck.

A few bumpy kilometres later, the truck slowed down and turned into a gate. It was dusk, the hour when the light played tricks on the eyes. Sid was glad they had reached. He had never been too comfortable riding at night. He pulled up and parked next to the truck just as Krish got down.

'Follow me,' Krish said and started to walk into what seemed like an orchard with rows of mango trees.

Sid slung his backpack over his shoulder. He could see tall coconut trees swaying in the breeze. A few bulbs flickered in the distance. The air had the faint scent of mangoes mingled with the fragrance of damp earth and wood smoke. Something about the place felt alive and yet mysterious, as if it held many secrets waiting to be discovered.

The path wound through the trees and more lights now emerged ahead. Against their backdrop, Sid could see the tall, athletic figure in front of him purposefully striding away. He picked up his pace and followed.

'Welcome and make yourself comfortable,' Krish said as they finally entered a large mud cottage. The stone flooring and terracotta-tiled roof caught Sid's attention immediately.

'Wow! I haven't seen this kind of construction too often,' he remarked.

'They don't make these kinds of buildings anymore. Come, let me show you the spare bedroom,' said Krish as he moved towards an open door and ushered Sid into his resting place for the night.

'The bathroom is attached. You should find the few things that you might need there. Dinner will be ready in thirty minutes, if you'd like to join me,' he said cheerfully and without really waiting for Sid to respond, disappeared into the back of the cottage.

As Sid stood under the shower and allowed the dust of the day to be washed away, he couldn't help but wonder at the turn of events. Here he was in a stranger's house, in the middle of nowhere, and somehow, it did not really feel out of place.

Dinner was a simple affair of salad and soup. Krish sat down at the small dining table and closed his eyes in prayer. Sid was not used to this and had never done anything like it, so he sat in silence waiting for his host to start the meal. 'Come, let's enjoy the food. I normally eat in silence, so please do not mistake my quietness for anything else,' said Krish as he opened his eyes and smiled at Sid.

'Thank you for your hospitality,' said Sid as he served himself a large portion of the freshest salad he had ever seen. The house was absolutely quiet. There was not a sound except for the background chirp of crickets as the two men ate their meal. Sid noticed that Krish closed his eyes after every bite, that he ate every mouthful very, very slowly—almost as if he were meditating on every ingredient in the salad.

Why did this have to happen? Will things improve tomorrow? Will I be able to get to a hotel by tomorrow night? Thank goodness I don't have anyone worrying about me. These and many more thoughts were going on in Sid's mind as he tried to enjoy the meal, but every few seconds his mind would again start its endless chatter.

Some time later, Sid realized he had eaten enough. Not wanting to seem rude, he continued sitting silently at the table while Krish finished his meal. At the end, after he had said another prayer with his head bowed, as if giving thanks for what he had eaten, Krish finally looked up.

'Come. Let's put our plates away and walk around a bit if you are not too tired, Sid,' he offered. As they stepped out into the cool breeze, Sid was struck by the freshness of the air and the clear skies.

'So, what's on your mind, my friend? You seemed really preoccupied as you ate. Want to talk about it?' asked Krish, turning towards Sid with a smile as he led them on a mud path that was intermittently lit by solar lanterns.

'Oh, not much,' said Sid. 'I was just thinking about how uncertain things have suddenly become for me. I had planned my trip well, but the road closure has just thrown a spoke in the wheel. I was thinking about how to work it out tomorrow.'

'Ah. I understand. You were so busy thinking about tomorrow that you forgot to taste your dinner today!' laughed Krish. There was something about the way he said it that Sid couldn't muster a response. Under most circumstances, he would have taken offence to being spoken to like this, but not now. There was an easy charm to this man.

'It's normal to be disturbed by uncertainty, don't you think? What would you do in such a situation?' Sid asked.

'Certainty is overrated,' said Krish, stopping by a little pond. In spite of the evening shadow, Sid could make out that it contained lotus plants. The surface was partly covered with the floating leaves with one stem raising its head above the surface. At its tip was a lotus bud.

As he stared at it, little did Sid know the significance it would have on his life. 'Tell me, what is certain?' Krish continued as he sat on a bench by the pond and patted it indicating that Sid should sit too.

'Was it certain that you would be born? What was the probability of your conception itself? One in a million? And then once you were born, did you know what you would study in university? Did you know the kind of career you would take up?'

'Well, not really.'

'For that matter, do you know whether you will even be alive tomorrow?'

'No, I don't, although I hope to be!'

'Imagine there is a new movie releasing. You have heard it is a superb suspense thriller and your favourite stars are acting in it. You book gold class tickets for the first show along with your friends. On the day of the show, there is much anticipation. You go to the theatre, buy popcorn and settle down in your seat to watch the movie. The movie starts. Now imagine that before every scene plays out on the screen, you know the outcome of the scene. You know every twist in the tale before it happens. How will you feel? Will you enjoy the movie? Will your popcorn taste good?'

'I guess not.'

'Why not? What is happening?' asked Krish

'I guess there is no suspense. I think what makes for a great movie is the unexpected twists and turns!' replied Sid 'If I know it all, I will get bored! Why would I even watch a movie like that? Leave alone paying good money to watch it?' laughed Sid.

'Precisely. There is no suspense. No thrill. It's boring! Now imagine if your life too was like that. Where everything was certain and you knew everything the way it was going to happen! How would it feel?'

'Pretty boring, I guess!' Sid laughed as he pictured his life the way Krish was describing it.

'Now that's interesting, isn't it? Especially coming from a man who was craving certainty just moments ago!' Krish laughed along.

'Now let's say you have gone trekking or mountain climbing or river rafting. What are you seeking there? Is it not the thrill of the unknown? How different is your road trip now, my dear friend? What is it but an adventure? An adventure, by definition, means you encounter surprises and challenges. There will be twists and turns in the plot as you, the protagonist, use the skills you need to navigate them skilfully.'

'When you put it like that, I totally see what you mean. I think life is and should be an adventure!' exclaimed Sid excitedly.

When you embrace uncertainty, it's called an adventure.
When you fight it, it's called fear.

'The only thing you can really be certain of is this moment. Just this present moment. As the saying goes, the past is history, the future is a mystery and that's why this moment is called the "present". It's the one thing gifted to you that you have full control over. Let me tell you a story to explain this better.

'One day, while walking through the wilderness, a man stumbled upon a vicious tiger. He ran but soon came to the edge of a high cliff. Desperate to save himself, he climbed down a vine that dangled over the fatal precipice. The tiger stopped at the edge. As the man hung there, two mice ventured out of a hole in the cliff and began gnawing at the vine! Surely it would snap soon. Suddenly, he noticed a plump wild berry growing on the vine. He plucked and popped it in his mouth. It was incredibly delicious!'

Krish paused as if the story was over. Sid filled in the silence.

'Ah! The analogy I get from this story is . . . the tiger is the past. And the cliff is the future. The two mice are like time which can slowly kill us. The berry is the present. Forget the past, do not worry about the future and concentrate instead on the present moment. Only then, we can live happily.'

'Yes. You have understood correctly. By deeply embracing each moment, life starts to feel like an adventure. And in living one moment after the other, you design your destiny! So, breathe. You are alive and have control over this moment. Make a choice. Make a difference. With certainty. And life will certainly take care of itself.

'And by the way, the man in the story found calm as he ate the berry. In that calm, he found clarity and had an idea. He spat the seed of the berry at the mice, scared them away and then climbed back up the cliff with the help of the vine as the tiger had gone by then.'

Sid chuckled at the ingenuity of what the man in the story had done.

'When faced with uncertainty, I sometimes find myself stressed and anxious. At other times I feel completely exhausted. I worry about certain things, avoid other things and even people. I feel vulnerable and afraid. But then there are times when I feel the excitement of uncertainty too! Especially when I ride my Harley. Would you help me understand how one thing called uncertainty makes me experience all these different emotions?'

'There are many, many questions within that question, my young friend,' Krish replied. 'There are many books devoted entirely to explaining each one of these emotions! But I have not read any of them so I will respond to you from a place of "not knowing",' he chuckled.

Everything you lose, creates space for everything you need!

'Let's start with stress—the first thing you mentioned. People keep saying there is a lot of stress in the world these days. Can you show me where it is? Stress is not in the supermarket. Stress is not something that is out there. Stress is what *you* produce in response to what is happening to you!

'When you think the situation is beyond your ability to cope, you start feeling stressed. A little bit beyond your ability can be good because it makes you stretch. But if you think it's well beyond your ability, your emotions trigger your body and mind to produce adrenalin and cortisol to help you deal with it. That is stress.

'An overwhelmed feeling is nothing but an extreme level of stress. It is a point where you almost feel unable to function. This is the exhaustion you mentioned.

'Worry is nothing but a chain of thoughts about how the future is going to be and imagining terrible things. Worry is an activity of the mind.

'Anxiety is what follows worry. The body reacts to that, and caffeine, alcohol and drugs are what people resort to as they try to cope. Instead, calm the mind, eat healthy, sleep well and exercise. You'll see these worries and anxieties fade away like the shadows at dawn.'

'Hmm. I can see how you mean that. I am also able to see how I ended up creating some of my own "coping" mechanisms,' said Sid thoughtfully.

'Avoiding certain things and certain people is also a way you cope with anxiety. To avoid what might be painful, we are capable of running from anything we perceive as a "threat"—blaming others and even shutting down all communication.'

The simplicity of Krish's explanations was striking. Sid had met many brilliant people in his life, but the clarity with which this man was explaining complex ideas was something Sid had not seen before.

What place of not knowing is this man operating from? Sid wondered as he saw Krish close his eyes and breathe deeply as if he was tapping into some reservoir.

'Let's look at vulnerability,' Krish continued. 'It is something that every living being experiences. It is the feeling we get when faced with a challenge, a risk, uncertainty. A seedling that has just sprouted is vulnerable, as is a newborn puppy and a person talking about their feelings. Unfortunately, vulnerability is often taught to us as a sign of weakness. I say the opposite. To be vulnerable takes immense courage. To accept that one is vulnerable and then embrace that sense of vulnerability and make choices in line with our values is wisdom.

'Fear can hold a lot of information too. Start by asking yourself if it is a real fear. For example, if you have to jump off the fourth floor of a building, the fear of breaking your bones is a real fear. But most times in life, we are not in such situations.'

**Our fears are mostly imaginary or perceived.
We are afraid of things that are not there and may
never even be there.**

Like another person's judgment of us!, thought Sid.

'When you feel fear, lean into it like you would into a curve on your motorcycle. Yes, there is an element of risk and danger, but when you trust your instincts and riding skills, you come alive.

'Adventure sports and extreme sports are the perfect example of this. Addictive in fact because of the hormones your body pumps.'

On the other side of fear, is aliveness.

As Sid's mind processed the depth of what Krish had just said, he glanced at the sky. After a few minutes of silence, Krish stood up. 'We should say good night now, my friend. You should perhaps get some sleep,' he said and slowly started walking back towards the cottage.

As Krish's words swirled in the stillness of the night, Sid remained seated, his thoughts racing surprisingly clearer than usual. He replayed the conversation in his mind—the way Krish had so easily untangled emotions like stress, worry and fear, reframing vulnerability as a strength. It was as though someone had held up a mirror, not to show him what he already knew, but to reveal what he hadn't yet understood about himself.

The idea of leaning into fear, like leaning into a bend on his bike, struck a deep chord. It wasn't about avoiding uncertainty or trying to conquer it. It was about feeling it fully, trusting his instincts and moving through it.

He watched the lotus bud as Krish's footsteps faded into the night. The sky above twinkled with stars. For a moment, the world felt both vast and intimate, like the universe had conspired to bring him here to have these conversations with this man.

When eventually Sid got up to follow him, he felt a strange energy along with a sense of calm. Where it came from, he was not fully certain. He had never met anyone like Krish before. There was something almost indescribable about him. His mere presence made you calm and when he spoke, it energized you and you wanted to listen.

That night, Sid picked up his journal. He had not been writing in it much or regularly. He had thrown it into his backpack almost as an afterthought.

He sat at the little table by the window and looked outside. In the distance, he could make out the outline of a large tree. Just outside his window, bamboo stalks waved in the wind.

As he stared at the lines on the page, he began recollecting and noting down Krish's words.

Day 1: An Adventure Called Uncertainty

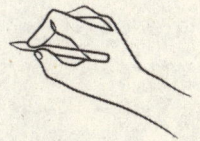

> Certainty is overrated.
>
> When you embrace uncertainty, it's called an adventure.
>
> If you fight it, it's called fear.
>
> A calm mind and staying in the present moment help you embrace uncertainty.
>
> Many of my fears are perceived fears and are imagined.
>
> Making choices based on these imaginary fears restricts me from living to my potential.
>
> I must lean into the fears like I lean into the bend in the road.
>
> Because when nothing is certain, anything is possible.
>
> And with skill and balance, I can then come alive!

As Sid wrote these few lines, he felt relaxed, at ease. After being discharged from the hospital two weeks ago, he had trouble sleeping but that night, he slept better than he had in a long time.

Day 2: Who Am I?: A Journey of Self-Awareness

Sid slept for ten hours straight. When he woke up, he could hear the birds and see sunlight streaming through the window of his room. He smelled the scent of wildflowers on the light breeze that fluttered the curtains.

As he stretched and lay in bed, there was a sense of anticipation. He smiled as he got up. The large tree in the distance was clearly visible now. The gnarly trunk, the bent branches spreading out like strong arms wanting to scoop up the earth before rising up into the sky.

He could faintly hear some music. It sounded like Dire Straits, one of his favourite bands. Drawn to it, Sid stepped out of the cottage and started walking towards a small shed-like structure where the music seemed to be coming from. As he rounded the bushes that surrounded the shed, he saw Krish. He was standing next to a large horizontal wooden wheel. Sid looked on curiously as Krish stood at the wheel, his body gently swaying to 'The Tunnel of Love'. He walked around the wheel and moved a few things away to a corner. He then came back with a pail of water. The morning breeze blew across Sid's face as he looked on, now more intently, wondering what Krish was doing. 'Someone his age and living alone should be sitting in a recliner with the newspaper and a cup of hot coffee,' thought Sid.

Krish continued his preparations and seemed completely oblivious to Sid's presence.

After a few minutes, he sat next to the wheel and folded his hands as if in prayer. Sid watched in fascination. After what seemed like ages, Krish opened his eyes and to Sid's surprise, turned to look directly into his eyes and smiled at him.

'Would you like to sit more comfortably and watch?' he asked Sid who was quite embarrassed that he had been caught staring so openly.

'I'm sorry, sir. I didn't mean to disturb you,' Sid said with a sheepish smile.

'No offence taken, my friend. I was just offering you a more comfortable seat.'

'But, why are you praying to a wheel?' asked Sid, emboldened by Krish's friendly tone.

'Come. Sit here,' said Krish as he gently poured what looked like oil into his hands and slowly rubbed them together.

Sid wasn't sure if he was going to get an answer.

He walked up and took the stool that Krish had pointed towards, only then noticing the pile of clay next to him.

'What do you see here, Sid?' asked Krish waving his hand around him.

'A potter's wheel, a stick, a pile of clay, a bucket of water, two stools to sit on and a piece of cloth,' said Sid, quite proud of his observant mind.

'And what else?' asked Krish gently as he used the stick to turn the wheel and give it momentum.

'The two of us, the garden . . . the cottage?' asked Sid a little more hesitantly now, not sure what the man was expecting to hear.

'Do you see nothing? Look at the centre of the wheel. Can you see nothing there?' asked Krish as he picked up the mound of clay with both hands and placed it at the centre of the wheel.

'Pay attention. Only then will you see it,' he continued as his hands slowly encircled what had a moment ago been a completely shapeless lump of clay.

'Attention is key,' he droned, almost as if he was dozing off.

Sid watched as if hypnotized. In front of his eyes, the shapeless lump of clay was transforming itself. Into a ball at first and then into a cup-like shape.

'Do you see it now?' asked Krish after what seemed like an eternity. 'There was nothing where the clay is taking shape now. It was just an empty space on top of the wheel.' He continued without waiting for Sid to answer. 'You were too focused on everything to see the empty space. To see the nothingness.'

The cup-like shape was now morphing into something that looked like a pot. 'I press too hard and we lose everything. I press too gently and we make no progress. But the right level of effort is giving meaning to nothing.'

'I am beginning to see what you mean, sir,' said Sid in awe. He had an inkling that maybe he was not just getting a lesson in pottery.

'It's the same with life, my friend,' came Krish's voice as if he was reading Sid's mind.

'Would you mind pouring us some tea?' Krish asked as he nodded towards a table on which sat an exquisite tea pot with two little cups next to it.

'Sure,' Sid said. It was almost as if Krish had been expecting him to join him. Everything was neatly laid out. He poured from the pot and a smile lit his face when he caught a whiff of jasmine. How did Krish know that he loved jasmine tea?

He picked up the cups and walked back quickly. He did not want to miss seeing the emptiness that was transforming in front of him.

'You see how one has to take away the clay in some places to allow for emptiness? And one then has to also keep the clay from filling that space up again? In doing this, we give meaning to the empty space.'

Sid watched as Krish deftly carved away at the rotating clay with one hand while smoothing it with the other. A beautifully-shaped pot had emerged already and now Krish was moving on to sculpting what was beginning to look like a spout.

'You need the same kind of effort in your life too. First remove all that is not required. Your fears, your anger, your hatred, your jealousy, your greed, your gluttony. And then keep them away. Just like we keep the clay from filling up that empty space again,' Krish continued as he reached one muddy hand out to pick up his tea.

Sid did not know if it was the steam rising from his cup or the light of the morning that reflected off the tea in it, but for a moment the scene in front of him seemed bathed in a golden-brown halo that made it seem unreal.

A few tears started to sting in his eyes as he thought back on his life. His fear of not being the best, the ambition to prove himself that had always motivated him, the fierce competitiveness that had driven him, the times he had not hesitated to use someone else's ideas as his own to fuel the next success. And even if his conscience had made the effort to remove these clumps of guilt, his mind had not allowed it. Tricky explanations had filled up the empty space again and the nothingness was lost.

'That's not all,' Sid heard Krish say, as he tore himself away from the painful memories that had made him teary-eyed.

'There is more to this' he said as he put aside the pot with the spout now added to it.

'Look.' He picked up more clay and started rolling it between his hands. 'Not only do you remove some things and keep them away, but you have to shape new things and keep adding them.'

As Sid watched, in a few short minutes, the short roll of clay had become an elegant strip. 'The handle!' exclaimed

Sid, completely engrossed by now in this little scene that was playing out.

'Excellent,' said Krish with a smile of encouragement as he picked up another little lump of clay and kept it under his hands on top of the wheel.

'Let's add to our awareness, love, kindness and compassion. Let's shape them into beautiful embellishments,' he said as his hands moved and revealed to Sid a small lid with a perfect round head.

'And when you take the effort to bring them all together, that is when you have something really meaningful,' he continued as he reached out for the pot with the spout and gently attached the strip to it. 'Remember, the secret lies in the amount of effort you put in. It's got to be right. Not too much as that can create too much stress and break things. Not too little as that does not create anything tangible.' He massaged the strip into the body of the pot as he spoke. Sid could now barely see where the pot ended and the handle began.

Krish stood up. He now had a lovely little teapot with a cheerful spout in his palm. With a flourish like a composer in an orchestra, he put the lid on it. 'This is almost ready. It needs to be baked. But before that, let's make it a bit more pretty.' And saying that, Krish pulled out a quill from his shirt pocket and went on to etch the surface of the pot with what seemed like a number of curved lines.

'We put in the right amount of effort to remove unwanted elements and then add more effort to keep them away, creating a space where even emptiness serves a wonderful purpose. Similarly, we made the effort to add new good things and then to keep them there, making the whole project even more meaningful.

'Now think about life for a minute. Were you making too much effort in life and trying too hard? Where do you try to grasp too much? What do you need to let go of? Can you think of them?

'On the other hand, where do you try too little? Where are you lazy? What are you afraid of?

'You know all these things. You just don't ask the right questions because you are afraid of what the responses might mean. Because the answers may tell you that you need to learn to balance. They may tell you that you need to make the effort. To rearrange. To put in more work in some places and let go in others. But then, that is the puzzle we are all born to solve. Either we can rearrange and grow in the process or just wait around for it to get rearranged. Everything gets rearranged anyway. It just takes longer, sometimes a few lifetimes, and it's not half as interesting as doing it yourself!'

Awareness is like the sun. When it shines on things, they are transformed.

'And finally, these little squiggles add an element of cheer to the whole package,' said Krish smilingly as he turned around to show Sid his creation. It was then that Sid realized that the 'little squiggles' were in fact music notes that had been etched into the pot!

Mark Knopfler was strumming 'Money for Nothing' in the background.

'Wow! This is amazing!' said Sid. 'You truly have an interesting way of looking at pottery and life. What would you say is the essence of this lesson?'

'Attention,' said Krish after a pause.

Day 2: Who Am I?: A Journey of Self-Awareness

'But I am listening,' insisted Sid. 'There must surely be a great deal more to having such a profound way of looking at life. Can you tell me the secret of that? And how I can practise it in life?'

'Attention,' Krish repeated.

That is the first and most fundamental aspect to a better life, to better leadership, to better relationships. Full and complete attention to the present moment. To the activity at hand. To the person with you.

Krish looked at Sid and smiled before picking up his freshly-crafted teapot and walking off into his cottage.

Sid leaned back, letting the story sink in. The breeze seemed to carry with it the weight of Krish's words.

'So, Krish,' he said eventually once he'd found Krish inside the cottage, his voice thoughtful, 'what you're saying is that the answers to those questions aren't really about finding some grand plan, but about staying present and doing what's needed in the moment?'

Krish smiled, his eyes twinkling with a quiet wisdom. 'Exactly. We seek certainty, a way to always make the "right" decisions. But life doesn't offer guarantees. The only power we truly have is in the now. The person in front of us, the task at hand—these are what matter.'

Sid nodded slowly, replaying the message in his mind. 'So, the most important time is always now. The most important person is whoever we're with at this moment. And the most important thing to do is to help them or do what's needed right then.'

'Precisely,' Krish said, pouring tea into a delicate clay cup. 'When we stop worrying about future outcomes and focus on the present moment, we unlock our ability to act meaningfully. We achieve this through action, not deliberation.'

Sid's gaze shifted to the horizon, the shades of light reflecting his deepening thoughts. 'This sounds a bit simplistic. I mean, I always feel like I need to plan everything, to make sure nothing goes wrong. Don't I need to take control, Krish?'

Krish chuckled softly, setting down his teapot. 'Planning isn't wrong, Sid. It's when we get trapped in overthinking—when our plans take us away from the now—that we lose balance.'

Sid sighed, feeling both the challenge and the simplicity of the lesson. 'So, it's about showing up fully, isn't it? For myself, for others and for the moment.'

Krish stood, placing a hand gently on Sid's shoulder. 'Yes. And remember, the answers to life's biggest questions often aren't in books or theories. They're in how you live each moment. And in living each moment fully, moment by moment by moment, we are continuously weaving the wonderful fabric called life. Now, let's enjoy some tea and let the day unwrap its own wisdom.'

As they shared the tea, Sid couldn't help but feel that a very different journey had begun—not on the road this time, but into himself.

It was afternoon by the time Sid packed his bag and got ready to leave. As he plonked his rucksack on the dining table and set off to say goodbye and thank Krish, he noticed a small brown carton on the table with his name written on it.

Inside, wrapped in shreds of newspaper was the most beautiful teapot he had ever seen. A beautiful sky blue with shades of white as if clouds were floating inside the pot. As Sid turned the pot, he discovered little musical notes, etched and painted in dark blue, that seemed to resonate with a life of their own. Tied to the handle was a little string with a note at the end. 'Life is like brewing a cup of tea. It's all about how you make it. Enjoy it!'

In that moment, another string tugged at Sid's heart.

Why have I been this way? he thought. *I have forgotten a number of basic things in my life. I don't pay attention to many things anymore. Both big and small. But since meeting this strange man yesterday, I have felt different. What is the message here? Is my life trying to tell me something? Was the road being closed a sign that I should open my mind? Am I like a lump of clay waiting to be moulded?*

Just then Krish walked in. It looked like he had been working outdoors as his sleeves and jeans were both rolled up.

'Hello, Sid!' he said cheerfully.

'Would it be okay for me to stay another night? It's afternoon already and it just might rain again. I'll set out early tomorrow morning.' Sid surprised himself as he suddenly blurted out and stood up with folded hands in an involuntary gesture.

Was it the sheer presence of this man or his own desperation that resulted in this plea? Sid did not know for sure.

'Of course. I've already cooked some food for you,' Krish said with a cryptic yet indulgent smile as if he had known all along that this was how things would play out.

* * *

That evening, Sid sought Krish out and found him brewing some tea in the small open kitchen.

A light shower had drenched the earth leaving behind the unmistakable fragrance of petrichor. A cool breeze carried the faint rustle of leaves with it. A naked bulb strung from the wooden beam on the ceiling cast its glow across the modest setup. A worn wooden table stood in one corner, its surface scattered with spice jars. The fragrance of tea mingled with the earthiness of the evening to create a moment of soft stillness. Sid paused for a moment, taking it all in—the simplicity, the calm—and felt a rare sense of peace settle over him as he stepped closer to Krish.

'I've been thinking about what you've said to me. It feels like something is missing in my life and at work. I think it has to do with me not paying attention to the right things. I would like to become more attentive, more self-aware. Can you help me?' he asked Krish.

Krish smiled as he poured the tea, his words deliberate and calm.

'Self-awareness, is a term we use casually, isn't it? We say things like, "That person has no self-awareness", or "I'm quite self-aware". But tell me—what does it really mean to be self-aware?'

He paused, letting the question linger before continuing.

'Imagine you've just bought a new smartphone. Wouldn't you take time to learn how it works? As advanced as that phone is, it's nothing compared to the most high-tech piece of equipment you'll ever encounter—yourself. Human beings are more intricate than the most complex supercomputer. Yet, how often do we take the time to understand our own instruction manual? The powerful truth is—we co-create the instruction manual. And yet, we spend so little time with it. Why do you think that is?'

Sid realized he had been right to come to Krish with his question. He waited patiently for him to continue.

'Let me share something fascinating. In an experiment, researchers asked people to sit in a room with nothing—no gadgets, no distractions. Just a table and a chair. At first, they simply sat there, but after a while, they noticed a button on the table. Out of curiosity, they pressed it.

'When they did, they got a mild electric shock. Now, what do you think happened next? Logically, you'd expect them to stop pressing the button, right? Who would willingly choose discomfort?

'But here's the surprising part—they didn't stop. They kept pressing the button, again and again. It turns out, they preferred to experience the shock rather than sit quietly with themselves! Think about that—what does it say about our ability to just *be* with ourselves?

'Now, I want you to also think about self-consciousness. It is different from self-awareness. Being self-conscious means I am very conscious of what others are thinking of me. It has very much to do with the exterior self. *How do people think I look, how do I speak, how do I come across*?

'On the other hand, self-awareness is about looking inwards. You ask questions such as "How do I see myself in a real way?" We all know people in our lives who are self-conscious. We have probably even criticized them. We say, "Look at that person, he or she is so awkward." What we are trying to say is that people who are self-conscious don't come across as very graceful.

'There are different ways in which self-consciousness comes across. One could be a need to show off oneself and one's possessions. Another could be shyness and social awkwardness. All this happens when we become very conscious of how others are perceiving us.

'On the other hand, if you look at somebody who is self-aware, there would be a certain grace about them even though they may have limitations about how they look and the things they own. And interestingly, it seems like there is an inverse correlation between these two. As self-consciousness increases, self-awareness reduces.

'So, if these are, in a way, opposites of each other, then what is self-awareness? It is nothing but the ability to see oneself from the inside, to understand your internal state in the present moment. *What are my priorities right now? What's going on in my mind? What's going on in my body? What is my intuition telling me?'*

Sid sat quietly, absorbing Krish's words. He began to piece it all together.

Self-consciousness, he thought, is all about the external—how I look, how I sound, what others think of me. It's like wearing a mask and constantly wondering how it appears to the world. And it's true, people who are overly self-conscious either try to show off or withdraw completely, trapped in others' perceptions. Self-awareness on the other hand is about turning inward. It's asking myself real, honest questions—What do I feel? What are my priorities? What's happening in my mind and body right now? It's not about seeking approval or avoiding judgment—it's about understanding oneself at that very moment.

'Now I am going to ask you, Sid: are you a self-aware person?'

Sid thought silently. He was deep in thought, thinking about everything Krish had said so far about self-awareness.

Before he could respond, Krish smiled and said, 'You don't have to give me an answer. Interestingly, when people are asked this question, 90 to 95 per cent say "yes". You may get variations of the answer, but the answer is "yes".

'However, when you ask the people around that person if they are self-aware, the percentage drops drastically. Only 10 to 15 per cent are considered self-aware by others around them. Isn't that a startling fact? That means more than 80 per cent of the people around you don't find you self-aware.'

Sid sat in silence, the weight of Krish's words settling on him. He realized that self-awareness wasn't something he could merely think about—it was something to be experienced through effort.

Krish's voice gently interrupted his thoughts, 'Let's explore this together, Sid. Shall we try a little practice to deepen your self-awareness?

'Take in a deep breath and check—what are the kind of thoughts that are going on in your head right now? Just observe, without being critical or judgmental, or even without having any expectations.'

Sid closed his eyes and took a deep breath. In his mind, he could see swirling clouds of thoughts—some about Krish's words, others darting to his plans for later. He observed them like clouds passing by in the blue sky, simply watching as they passed by, without holding on to any of them.

'On the second breath, ask yourself, "What's going on in my body right now?" Are you feeling bored right now or is there a sense of dullness? Are you confused about what I'm saying and is that causing restlessness? Or are you excited, curious, or even sleepy? Just observe.'

As Sid took a second deep breath, his awareness shifted to his body. He noticed a slight tension in his shoulders, a restless tapping of his foot and a faint heaviness in his eyes. He wasn't sure if it was confusion or curiosity—but he simply observed it all, letting the sensations be.

'On breath three, observe, "What kind of feelings do I have right now?" This is checking in with your heart. Look deeply into your heart and see what you notice.'

With his third breath, Sid turned his focus inward, towards his heart. He noticed different emotions—uncertainty, a hint of curiosity and also a faint glow of hope. He did not try to change any of them. He just observed them and sat with them. A little later, Sid softly opened his eyes. He felt like he had looked inside himself and seen only the tip of an iceberg. A beginning, nevertheless.

'Most people introspect to become self-aware. We ask ourselves "Why am I like this?", "Why did I behave like this?" or "Why did somebody else say or do that?"'

'Is that not true?' Krish asked.

Sid nodded. In fact, this was exactly what he had asked himself after he had collapsed due to burnout. He had wondered why and lost himself in the explanations conjured up by his mind.

Krish smiled at him knowingly and continued, 'Now, the problem is with the question you are asking. It is not with the process. Reflection and introspection are good for you.

But the problem is with the question, "Why am I like this?" It allows your mind to take over. Your mind will give you a detailed explanation, but one which may be quite removed from reality, from the truth.

'The mind is very clever. It will trick you into believing what it wants you to believe. In fact, it will try to make you believe that which further fuels its own existence! That you are fine just the way you are. Most times, it will convince you that the problem lies somewhere else. You end up reasoning that perhaps you behaved like that because a certain person said something wrong to you.'

There is no truth. There is only perception.

'So, what do we do instead? Ask yourself what happened in that situation? This is the more accurate way of introspecting or reflecting. And this is where something like mindfulness or awareness comes in.'

Sid rested his elbows on his knees, his hands loosely clasped as he stared at the floor, deep in thought. It's not reflection or introspection that's the issue—*it's the question I ask*, he realized. *Why am I like this?* only gave his mind room to create excuses, shifting blame and distorting reality. Instead, he needed to ask "What?"—*what is happening within me right now?* That's where mindfulness will come in, helping him see clearly without judgment.

He straightened up and met Krish's gaze, a quiet determination in his eyes, ready to explore this shift in perspective.

*Ask not why but **what**.*
***What** did I do in that moment?*

What *did I say in that moment?*

'This does not allow your mind to make up excuses and alternative realities for what happened. Behaviour, more than words, is a better indicator of what someone is thinking. We all know people who sometimes say one thing but behave in a completely different way. We then find it better to go by their behaviour rather than their words, isn't it? For example, you might be in a relationship where your partner says you are special to them. But they keep demonstrating abusive patterns and hurting you. Wouldn't you at some point say "Enough! I can't take this anymore."? Hence, behaviour is often a better indicator of what is going on inside a person.

'Asking why an incident happened leads to a lot of analysis, which creates so many different options that you lose yourself.'

Any area of your life where you find unintended consequences is an opportunity to practise awareness.

Krish's words lingered in the air, weaving clarity through the complex web of Sid's thoughts. The air was still, as if urging Sid to process the simplicity of the message.

Sid sat forward, his brow furrowed in deep thought as he tried to piece it all together. 'So, what you're basically saying is that our actions speak louder than words. Both to others and to us. So, if someone says they care about you but their actions keep hurting you, their behaviour eventually reveals the truth that they actually don't care enough. You can't ignore what they're showing you, right? Similarly, my own actions can give me a deep insight into myself. And instead of getting caught up in the endless "Why did this happen?", I should shift my awareness to focus on "what".'

Sid looked up at Krish, a sense of clarity dawning on him. 'It's about cutting through the clutter in the mind and seeing reality for *what* it is, isn't it?'

'Absolutely. And a very powerful way to do this is through journaling. Taking up simple prompts and then continuing to write whatever comes to mind. For example, you could start the journaling reflection with something like "When I feel happy, I . . . " or "When I feel angry, I . . ." and write focusing on not just thoughts and feelings, but behaviour. Over a period of time, this will help you develop a high-res image of yourself.'

We see things as we are. Not as they are!

Sid remembered having read this somewhere. It made complete sense now. He closed his eyes, trying to absorb the concepts Krish had spoken about. He said, 'I'm beginning to understand the difference, but how do I apply this to my life?'

Krish's eyes seemed to flicker in the light of the single bulb. He said, 'Let me tell you a story.'

There was an old Zen master. He was a very wise old man like most Zen masters are and he used to live a very simple life in his little hut, somewhere in the mountains. He had become very famous because of his wisdom and simplicity. Once, the king of a nearby kingdom heard about him and decided to pay him a visit. The king himself was well-known for his conquests in battle and his valour. He was a samurai, well-versed in the martial arts. There were many stories about how he had killed a hundred men single-handedly.

He decided to meet the Zen master because he had a burning question. So, he took a small group of troops with him and travelled by horseback to the Zen master's cottage. The Zen master was inside, getting ready for his evening meditation. Some of his disciples were outside sweeping, watering the plants and preparing for the master's meditation.

The king got down from his horse and went towards the cottage. One of the students met him and asked, 'May I help you?' The king replied, 'Do you know who I am? I am the king of the neighbouring kingdom and I have come here to meet your master because I have a very important question to ask.'

The student replied, 'If you don't mind, he is just getting ready for his evening meditation. Can you wait?'

The king was impatient and used to commanding respect. He said, 'No, no I cannot wait because I have to go back. Maybe you can ask him the question if he is busy? Just ask him and tell me what he says.'

The student said. 'Okay, I will try.'

The king said, 'Please go and ask him, what is heaven and what is hell?' When the student went inside, the master was just beginning to close his eyes.

The student exclaimed, 'Excuse me master, I am very sorry, a king has come to see you and he wants to ask you, "What is heaven and what is hell?"'

The master, without opening his eyes, replied, 'Ask him to look inside,' before he entered into a meditative state.

The student went outside and narrated the answer as he had heard it: 'Master has asked you to look inside.'

The king assumed he had to look inside the cottage. So, he went in and saw the master sitting there with his eyes closed.

He waited for a few minutes, thinking 'Maybe there is something here that the master wanted me to see that will give me the answer.' He looked around the simple mud cottage but saw nothing of importance. He walked around the room but when he still found nothing, he got annoyed. He thought the old man was fooling him.

He shouted, 'Hey, old man, are you making a fool of me? I asked you what is heaven and what is hell and you asked me to look inside. There is nothing here.'

The master slowly opened his eyes and said, 'I should have known that a man like you would not understand. You have got such strong muscles and you are such a great warrior, but at the end of it you are a complete idiot. What is the point in you being the king?' He went on berating the king.

The king listened quietly at first, but when the master did not stop, he became furious. Eventually, he unsheathed his sword and put it to the master's neck, ready to cut it off. Then the Zen master looked at him and said, 'This, my king is "hell".' And in that moment the king realized the weight of the master's comment.

He realized that hell was not a place, but a state of mind. He was so overcome by remorse and love and compassion in that moment for the old man that he started to weep. He begged forgiveness from the Zen master. Again, the master looked at him and said, 'Now this is "heaven".'

'Heaven and hell are not some places we go to after we die. No, heaven and hell are very much available right now. With self-awareness we can make the choice of where we want to be!' said the master to the king.

The trees rustled as a gust of wind blew through them as if it too had understood.

Heaven is not another place.
Heaven is not another time.
Heaven is being fully present. Right here. Right now.

'I think I'm beginning to understand now,' said Sid. 'In fact, what you've just said to me reminds me of the many instances where I have let my anger take me to hell. And while I certainly have had glimpses of heaven too, I can honestly admit that I could do with more of it!'

'Absolutely! You see, Sid, much like heaven and hell, the state of our mind depends on the thoughts and emotions we choose to nurture. The power to decide lies within us.' Krish smiled at Sid.

'And that power,' he continued, 'is accessible right NOW. If we are asked about the most wonderful moment of our lives, many say that it is yet to come. Some of us say that we have already experienced it, but many keep living with the expectation that it is on the way. If we continue living the same way that we have lived until now, we can be sure that moment will never arrive and then it is time for death. But when we are alive in the present moment, we can embrace all the wonders in life. If we can embrace the present moment, we can realize that it is the most wonderful moment, so that at the time of death, there is no regret that we never really lived at all. The Dalai Lama was once asked about what surprised him the most about humanity and he quickly responded, "Man!" He went on to say, "Because he sacrifices his health in order to make money. Then he sacrifices money to recuperate his health. And then he is so anxious about the future that he does not enjoy the present; the result being that he does not live in the present or the future; he lives as if he is never going to die, and then dies having never really lived.'"

They both quietly sipped their tea, with Sid lost deep in thought.

* * *

That night, Sid picked up his journal again.

He wanted to crystallize his learnings from that day. A cool breeze blew in, carrying with it the faint scent of wildflowers.

The bamboo leaves rustled as if to contribute their insights to Sid.

He began writing.

The ability to pay attention is key. It allows you to calm the mind. And with calm, comes clarity. We are then able to see things not just as we are, but as THEY are!

The most important moment is NOW. The past is history. The future is not here yet and so the ONLY moment we have any control over, is the present moment.

Ask not why but what. What did I do in that moment? What did I say in that moment? Observing behaviour is a better way to achieve self-awareness than merely analysing a situation mentally.

Self-awareness is inversely correlated to self-consciousness. One is inward focused while the other is outward.

In order to let come, you have to let go.

Day 2: Who Am I?: A Journey of Self-Awareness 47

My little practice:

Step 1: As I breathe in and out, I check in with my body.

Step 2: As I breathe in and breathe out, I check in with my thoughts.

Step 3: As I breathe in and breathe out, I check in with my feelings.

Reflection questions:

What are three of my superpowers?

How can I make the best use of them?

What areas of my life do I struggle to accept?

What would the people close to me say is the driving force in my life? What would I want it to be?

What is one thing I should start doing and one thing I should stop doing?

Even as Sid wrote these lines in his journal, he felt a sense of calm and clarity washing over him. Sleep beckoned.

Day 3: Meeting the Ghosts of Self-Criticism

The next morning Sid woke up early, feeling fresh. He noticed he was no longer relying on an alarm to wake up or get out of bed. Maybe it was because of the simple nourishing food he was eating at Krish's.

His mind went back to everything he and Krish had discussed the previous day. As he got out of bed, he tried to bring his awareness to every small task. He found his mind wandering constantly. By the time he was ready to step out, he was feeling quite dejected.

He stepped out of his room looking for Krish.

Day 3: Meeting the Ghosts of Self-Criticism

As Sid stepped into the garden, the cool morning breeze greeted him, carrying the earthy scent of freshly turned soil and dew-kissed plants. He spotted Krish amidst the greenery, his movements deliberate and calm as he tended to the weeds and watered the plants. For a moment, Sid paused, observing Krish's quiet focus. The contrast to his own restless thoughts felt stark.

Sid took a deep breath and started walking towards Krish.

Krish looked up at him. 'You seem to have slept well,' he remarked with a smile.

'Thank you. I've slept a lot better the last two nights than I have in the last few months,' Sid replied. 'I couldn't help but think about our conversation yesterday. I've been trying to be mindful of each task and more self-aware of my emotions and my physical self in each moment, but I find that my mind wanders after focusing for a short while. I soon start getting negative thoughts and am unable to focus. I'm not sure I'm cut out for this.'

Krish smiled at Sid. 'We all have a negative voice inside that judges us. We don't always need other people to criticize us. This voice is always there, even when you wake up in the middle of the night. It can keep you awake for hours, telling you about the mistake you made years ago. How you are not good enough. Even in our interactions, we remember negative comments more than positive conversations. This tendency is called negativity bias. It's a psychological aspect of all human beings.

Sid's gaze fell to the ground as Krish's words sank in. 'You're right,' he said softly. 'I remember this one time at work when I presented a big project to the leadership team. Everyone praised my ideas and the effort I'd put in, but one person pointed out a flaw in the data. It wasn't even a major issue, but that was all I could think about for days. The praise faded into the background and all I could recollect was that one comment telling me I wasn't good enough.'

He sighed, rubbing the back of his neck. 'Even now, when I think about it, I feel a pang of embarrassment, like I failed. And I know it's ridiculous because that project was a success.'

Sid looked at Krish, as if searching for an answer. 'Why is it that the negative sticks to us like glue while the positive just slides off?'

'When we were still evolving as human beings thousands of years ago, we lived in an environment where our survival was always threatened by predators. Our brains were attuned to this constant danger. A part of the brain, called the amygdala, is responsible for our survival. It is like a sentry, a gatekeeper to our brain. Based on our ecosystem, the brain became conditioned to react in one of three ways: fight, flight or freeze. When we were constantly threatened by predators, we could not afford to make a mistake.

'This survival instinct was so strong that we became very aware of our mistakes. This got hardwired into our brains as we evolved. So even today, this tendency is present in our brains as a negativity bias. But if we become aware of this, we can retrain our brains.'

Krish picked up a small pair of shears and peered intensely at a rose bush as he paused. He carefully pruned a few stems before stepping back to inspect his work.

'Let me explain with an example,' he continued. 'When you decide to buy anything new, let's say a car, you do some research. Eventually, you decide to buy a Honda. As soon as you make the decision, you will start noticing a lot of Hondas on the road. Suddenly it will seem to you like there are many Hondas.

'It is not that suddenly the number of Hondas on the road increased from the moment you decided to buy one. It's just that you started noticing them more. So, what you think is what you see around you!

'Now, bring this perspective to what I just said earlier. If a lot of your thinking is already negative, you will find more negative situations in life. It's a double whammy.

'As humans, we tend to remember traumatic experiences more than positive ones. We recall insults better than praise and think about negative things more frequently than positive ones. We wake up at night with regrets, "Oh my God, why did I do that? What will happen next? I shouldn't have done that."

'This kind of thinking triggers an inflammatory mechanism in the body as certain hormones are released due to repetitive negative thoughts. When you think happy thoughts, you feel light in the body. Your head goes up, your shoulders open out and you feel strong. The moment something bad or negative happens, the head falls, your shoulders droop, your body slumps and inside, other physiological reactions kick in even though you can't see them. Prolonged exposure to this state or negative hormones can be very harmful.'

Sid shifted uneasily, his gaze fixed on a patch of sunlight filtering through the trees. Krish's words echoed in his mind, drawing out memories he'd tried to bury. He thought back to a meeting six months ago—one of the countless high-stakes moments leading up to his burnout.

He'd walked into the boardroom, already carrying the weight of a sleepless night. A client presentation loomed, but he couldn't shake the sharp sting of criticism from his boss the previous evening. 'This report doesn't reflect leadership, Sid'—the words had played on a loop in his mind, dragging his confidence into the ground.

A team member had come in a bit late that morning and that had been enough to set Sid off. His cutting and sharp reprimand had created unease in the room. The meeting itself was not smooth, his tone defensive as he'd struggled to stay focused. He remembered leaving the room feeling drained, with a heavy chest and a pounding head. Sid sat on the rock, drawing patterns in the mud with a stick.

'Krish,' he began, 'it's like you're describing me from some time ago. I was stuck in this loop of negativity—one bad thought led to another and soon it was all I could see. It wasn't just affecting my mind; it was clearly breaking down my body too.'

Krish nodded knowingly, his voice calm and steady. 'That's the nature of it, Sid. Negativity is hardwired into us at the level of the brain. While it has an evolutionary advantage, this negativity bias can easily compound itself—mentally, emotionally and physically. It can become a cycle, and without awareness, it can spiral completely out of control. Let's talk about why this happens and how it impacts us, so we can learn how to break free.

'To start with, constant negative thinking impacts your productivity in a big way. Imagine negative hormones regularly being pumped into your body—what will happen? Disease will follow. Where does stress come from? It is not something that somebody comes and puts into your pocket; stress is your response to things.

'Negative thinking creates negative behaviours, which in turn creates more negative thoughts. One feeds into the other and we constantly keep going through this cycle. The same kind of thoughts produce the same results.'

'But what do I do if there is a pattern of negative thoughts that repeats itself?' Sid asked.

'I'm going to ask you a question. If there is darkness, what do you do? How do you control the darkness? Do you try to suppress it? No. You switch on a light or you light a candle. Similarly, there's no need to try to control or suppress negative thoughts. We are wired in a certain way. These thoughts do come and they have their own value. The danger is in the patterns that you mentioned. We lie awake at night, ruminating over and rehashing the same thoughts again and again. When that happens, you just need to become more aware. See, mindfulness is like a light in that darkness. It is a state of mind. When we develop that state of awareness, it automatically reduces these kind of thoughts.'

Sid frowned slightly, letting Krish's words sink in. The idea that his thoughts could influence his physical and mental health wasn't new to him, but hearing it framed so starkly made him feel the weight of its truth. He thought about the many restless nights he used to have, his mind full of thoughts, the constant self-doubt and how it all seemed to spiral into a cycle he couldn't escape.

'So, if our thoughts shape our reality, how can we stop this cycle of negativity and shape a different, more positive reality?' Sid asked, his voice tinged with curiosity.

Krish smiled, sensing the opportunity to guide him further. 'How do you think we can break out of this?' he asked, leaning forward slightly, his tone both probing and encouraging.

'Do we change our thoughts and think more positively?' Sid said hesitatingly.

'Positive thinking is one powerful way. And I am going to show you another way too. But first, let me tell you a story.

> There was a man named John. Now John used to work nine to ten hours a day. A hard-working chap. One day, he happened to be speaking to his manager and said, 'Life is so hard.' Guess what happened? The manager decided John needed to be sent to a positive thinking training programme.
>
> In the programme the trainer urged John, 'Can you do it?' as he taught the participants to shout back, 'Yes, I can do it.'
>
> John came back from the programme full of positivity. He worked very hard and, in a few years, he became the manager of his department. But you know what happened next? Johnny boy had to work fourteen hours a day!

Krish burst into laughter as he said this. 'Positive thinking can have a few limitations because sometimes it makes you lose sight of reality. It takes you to one end of the spectrum and, as long as everything is going well, it's great. But let's say things don't work out that way, not once but twice, three times. How often can you thump your chest and say, 'I can do it'? The second time your voice will drop a little bit, the third time you might still say 'I can do it', the fourth time you might say, 'No, I can't do it'.

'What you may need, is a supplement in your tool kit of life. Self-compassion. Compassion towards oneself.'

Sid had smiled at Krish's story, but the smile quickly gave way to thoughtfulness. He leaned back against a tree and stared at the sky. 'So, positive thinking isn't a magic wand,' he said, piecing things together. 'It's useful, but it can push you to ignore reality if you're not careful. It's like Johnny—he worked harder, climbed the ladder, but ended up stuck in a bigger hamster wheel.'

Sid exhaled slowly, reflecting on his own tendencies to push through challenges by doubling down on positivity, often at the expense of his well-being. He remembered the countless 100-hour weeks he had put in because long hours and stress had seemed like indicators of upcoming success. 'Maybe that's what I've been doing too. Forcing optimism to mask the real issues.'

Krish nodded. 'Exactly, Sid. That's where self-compassion comes in. It's not about masking reality but facing it with kindness and awareness. Let me explain how it works.

'There are some aspects to self-compassion. The first part is mindfulness. Mindfulness makes you aware. It gives you clarity of what exactly is going on. You become aware of yourself, aware of things around you. What you are thinking, how you are feeling and so on.

'The second aspect is a recognition that you are not alone. We forget that in that moment that there are many others also who are in the same boat. We think "Oh, why me? I am the only one in the whole world who has this problem." That is not true. Just looking around with awareness, we can see many others who might have worse troubles and have even overcome those. Just bringing this perspective into mind can help us work with our challenges better.'

Krish paused for a bit before launching into another story.

Once there was a man who had a lot of regrets. Every night when he went to bed, he would pray to God, 'Please take away all my troubles, give me somebody else's place in life. At least for one day, can you take away all my troubles and let me be somebody else? Anybody else. It doesn't matter because I think anybody has a better life than I do. Oh God! Help me, for my life sucks.'

Every night he would appeal to God. He would then try to sleep, tossing and turning, thinking about how he was no good. Finally, out of sheer fatigue, he would fall asleep. One night in his sleep he heard a voice that said, 'Tomorrow morning, take all your regrets and all your troubles and put them in a bag and come to the town centre.' He woke up in the morning and was thrilled, 'Finally, God has heard my prayers.' He did as he was told but on the way, he was surprised to see that he wasn't the only one heading there. He saw many other people with big bags all headed to the town hall. His neighbour, who owned an expensive SUV and a huge house had two big suitcases of his own.

The man got very worried. 'Should I even go? What's happening here? Why are so many people coming with such large suitcases and bags?' he wondered. Eventually, he thought to himself, 'Okay, let me go and see'. Once everybody had assembled in the hall, the booming voice of God told them to put their bags down.

'Now pick up any other person's bag that you want to keep for yourself and leave,' God continued. You know what happened? Everybody rushed and grabbed their own bags because they looked at the other bags and thought, 'I don't even know what kind of scary problems the other guy might have had. So, my problems might be better.'

So, they all picked up their own bags and rushed back home. When this man left to go back home, he was smiling. He saw a lot of other people smiling too. They were all happy that at least, they had only their own problems.

Sid couldn't help but smile again at Krish's story. The image of people scrambling to reclaim their own burdens struck a chord with him. He ran a hand through his hair, leaning back against the tree.

'So, we all carry our own bags of troubles,' Sid said thoughtfully. 'And as much as we might wish to trade them away, there's comfort in realizing that we're not alone in our struggles. Everyone is carrying something, even if it's invisible to us.'

He paused, reflecting on his tendency to isolate himself in his moments of self-criticism. 'It's funny, though. In those moments of self-doubt or regret, it always feels like I'm the only one in the world who's messed up. Like my problems are somehow unique.'

Krish nodded, his expression encouraging. 'That's exactly the trap, Sid. It's easy to forget that we're all human, navigating the same messiness of life. But once you start noticing this, it changes the way you approach your challenges—and yourself. You become a bit kinder to yourself.

'We think we are the only ones who have problems. We are the only ones who have made mistakes. This is far from the truth. The fact is, we are all human. We all make mistakes—some of us even make the same mistake many times.

'In moments of extreme self-criticism, it's good to bring mindfulness to the situation. To become aware: "This is what is going on and this is how I am feeling. What can I do better? What can I learn from others? What can I change? And if nothing, how can I become more accepting of what I can't change?"

'The third aspect of self-compassion is kindness. After you realize you are not alone, what do you do?

'Imagine this, your friend has made a mistake or something in their life has not gone too well. For example, they tell you: "I didn't get the promotion or I didn't get a raise this year." What would your response be? Would you kick them or slap them and say, "You are a loser. I told you, you don't deserve to get that"?'

'No, I wouldn't! That would be rather brutal. I'd probably try to be supportive,' said Sid, frowning as he pictured doing what Krish had just said.

'Exactly. You would perhaps say, "It's okay. You know you can always work harder and get it next time. Don't feel so bad." You would try to console them. But when it comes to yourself, why don't you do that?

'So you tell yourself, "It's okay, all is well. Don't worry, everything is going to be fine." You just give yourself a little bit of kindness. The fourth part of self-compassion, and here

I am borrowing a little trick from positive thinking, is called cognitive reframing. Cognitive is "of the mind" or "of the brain". We use our mind to reframe. So, let's say you are extremely sensitive to criticism. That might also mean that you have a very strong desire to improve, right? People who are very sensitive to criticism are likely to be perfectionists. They don't like anyone pointing a finger at them.

'Similarly, what does impatience tell you? That somebody also wants to be more efficient. They want to do something quickly. So, cognitive reframing is just a shift in perspective that allows you to see a situation in a slightly more positive way. Instead of beating yourself up, I am so impatient, you say, my impatience is the sign that I want to do things better, sooner and it's a sign of wanting more efficiency.'

As Krish explained, Sid started to see how he could have approached his setbacks differently. He had a tendency to be excessively critical—both of others and himself—and he could now see how that might have limited his growth. He closed his eyes for a minute and took a few deep breaths. Krish had paused as if to give Sid this space of deep reflection.

Eventually, he continued, 'With all that background Sid, I would like you to see how self-compassion can work. Think of a situation from your life. It could be personal or professional. Think of a recent failure. Once you think of the situation, just put it aside in your mind. We will revisit it a little later. Now let's start doing an experiment. Let us get into a state of mindfulness.'

Sid was ready. Shadows danced on the ground as the warm morning sun filtered through the trees. A gentle breeze blew across, carrying a faint scent of watered earth. A bird chirped melodiously. Krish gestured for Sid to sit under the shade of the large mango tree. The ground beneath them was cool and slightly damp, a reminder of nature's constant presence. 'Make yourself comfortable,' Krish said softly, his voice blending with the soothing rhythm of the environment. Sid crossed his legs and adjusted his posture, feeling the solid earth beneath him.

Krish closed his eyes briefly, taking in a deep, deliberate breath. Sid mirrored him, inhaling the calm of the surroundings. The breeze had slowed down but the leaves still rustled. The bird had stopped its chirping. It felt like time was pausing in its flow.

'Let's begin,' Krish said, his voice steady and calm. 'Focus on your breath. Let it anchor you to this moment. The past and the future can wait—right now, it's just you, your breath and this present moment.

'Start by noticing your posture and then take a few deep breaths. Notice that you breathe deeply on the inhale, allowing your body to expand. On the exhale, allow your body to relax.

'Breathe normally now. Notice the breath, focussing on the beginning of the inhale, the sensation as the breath goes in. Notice how it ends, then the beginning of the exhale, how the breath goes out. Notice there is a gap at the end of the inhale before the exhale begins and another gap after the exhale ends.

'Take that awareness now to your body. Notice how it feels as you are sitting here. If you wish to make any adjustments to your posture, notice the movement by taking your complete awareness to the body, allowing your entire awareness to fill up with the body. Notice your feet on the ground, the contact with the floor and using your awareness, identify any tightness or tension in the body. Become aware of the lower legs, the calf muscles, then the upper legs, noticing the weight of the body going into the ground. Notice the lower back, middle back, upper back, neck and shoulders. Use your awareness to soften and dissolve any tightness or tension in the body.

'Finally, take your awareness to your face, allowing it to soften and relax. Soften the forehead, relax the jaws and your tongue. Take your awareness now to the entire body, noticing that the body is a lot more relaxed now. Then take your awareness to the mind, noticing that it is calmer and more relaxed.

'Now in this state of awareness, recall the recent example of your failure. Bring it to mind again and first gently reflect on it in a state of mindfulness or awareness. What exactly happened? What were the circumstances around it that led to the so-called failure?'

Sid thought about a project where the client had given them a poor rating.

'If there were other people involved, without blaming or judging anything or anybody, just notice who and what other factors might have had a role to play in that outcome. Do you think you might be the only one who faced a situation like that? What might have happened with the others?'

One of the consultants had made a mistake while accounting for some data, which had impacted the whole project. They had all worked on extremely tight deadlines, though. Sid had missed it in the final report and the client was not happy at the end.

'What you can learn perhaps is that you are not alone in this. Be compassionate towards yourself. Think kindly towards yourself. Explore if there is any reframing of the situation that might be possible for you. Is there a way of seeing it from another perspective, a slightly gentler and kinder one? Emotions have information in them. Check in with your body to see if it can give you any other information that can shape your perspective.

'Now let go of the whole memory, all the thoughts and emotions around it. Take your awareness back to the breath. Notice the inhale and the exhale as well as the spaces in between. There is nowhere else to be right now, nothing else to do, simply resting in awareness, not getting attached to any thoughts or emotions. Just be the observer.

'Whenever you are ready, softly open your eyes.'

Sid opened his eyes, feeling as if a small weight had been lifted.

'Don't let this meditation be a one-time thing. Take it further. Write a letter to yourself from the perspective of a dear friend or a mentor. What would they say to you about this challenge and how you dealt with it? What would they say to you about the opportunities in your life?'

Sid pondered. He thought back to all the people who had always called him a winner. What would they say to him now?

Krish continued, 'When you go back to your room, try and write this in the form of a letter: "Dear Sid, I know that these are the challenges and opportunities you are facing right now. I would like to tell you that . . ." and you just continue writing and see what comes up.

'If you are thinking, "Won't this make me complacent?", I only want to ask you, "Why do we think that we should not be self-compassionate? Why do we feel the need to push ourselves harder?" Because we believe that it will lead to a drop in performance. It will reduce motivation, won't it? Now, this is what we have been told through conventional education and social norms. Right through growing up, we've been told, "Come on, you need to push yourself some more."

'I am not against pushing some more. Only against pushing blindly. The secret of self-compassion is knowing where to push, when to push and how much to push. I'll talk about some studies in this area.

'In a study conducted by Juliana G. Breines and Serena Chen, they divided their subjects into three groups. One group of people were all positive thinkers. They were all taken to a workshop and trained in positive thinking for two weeks. The second group was more of a control group. They were not told anything. They were just taken to a workshop and left alone to do their own stuff. The third group was taught self-compassion practices exactly like what we did now. They were taught a few practices. At the end of two weeks, the researchers found something really interesting.

'The popular expectation would have been that the positive thinking group would have been the ones to come out on top. Instead, they found that the group that practised self-compassion did the best. Instead of reducing performance, self-compassion brought about a very balanced perspective to the participants. It prevented burnout while improving their performance in a very healthy way.

'They also found that it does not reduce your motivation to succeed. Again, very counter-intuitive because a lot of people think that being kind to yourself means you will not have the motivation to achieve great things. Not true. It created healthy motivation, contrasted with positive thinking, which can be an extreme form of motivation.

'If, like a pendulum, you go to one end of motivation, the chances are that at another time, you will go to the other end too. That is the law of nature. The pendulum cannot always stay in one place. So, if you keep practising positive thinking, chances are that if things don't work, you could also feel disappointment more keenly.

'On the other hand, self-compassion creates healthy motivation based on mindfulness. It is contingent on who you are, the circumstances and your emotions. So, it's almost like doing an analysis of yourself with a very calm, balanced mind.

'Interestingly, there was another hypothesis that people with self-compassion might compromise on their ethics. The theory was that they might do something slightly unethical and then apply self-compassion to it and say, "It's okay. You did it because of whatever reasons; it's okay to be unethical sometimes."

'What the researchers found was that because of the awareness, there was a higher degree of honesty, compared to the people who practised positive thinking. Positive thinking sometimes, with the goal-obsession that it creates, can create an ethical transgression. That means you compromise a little bit on ethics because you are going towards your goal in such a focused manner.

'Counter-intuitive to what you think, self-compassion does not reduce performance, motivation, effort or ethics. In fact, it increases many performance parametres, which are extremely useful in today's circumstances. It brings about a greater sense of balance and consistency to the way you operate.

'In the world we live in, there is so much negative news around us that we are attuned to look for negatives. Self-compassion with mindfulness can create a growth mindset because it makes you aware of your negativity bias and therefore makes you able to bring more awareness to understanding what's going on and say, "Ah, I am being too hard on myself right now; I'm being too self-critical."

'Positive thinking, which can motivate you to do impossible stuff, also puts a lot of pressure on yourself. Self-compassion is a gentler way. It allows us to fix past errors. In our positive efforts, we may become so charged up to make things work that we can forget about fixing some of the errors of the past. Self-compassion also makes you realize, "Ah, maybe I haven't been too good at something" or maybe "I haven't been very kind in a certain situation to a certain person" and it allows us to even go back and fix them. It means that in a recurrence of such situations we would be much more well-equipped to bring about a positive outcome going forward. So, contrary to what one might initially think, self-compassion has a number of benefits.

'I want you to remember that I'm not replacing positive thinking; I am offering you the technique of self-compassion as a supplementary strategy. Positive thinking doesn't always work because there are only so many things that you can control and a lot of things you can't.'

Sid looked thoughtful as he asked, 'But how do I practise self-compassion on a daily basis?'

Krish nodded and said, 'That's a good question. I am going to offer you a little micro-practice. This might help you in difficult situations. At times we all feel overwhelmed, "Oh, there's just so much to do! How do I manage?" We even need to tell people difficult things sometimes. They don't make us terribly popular and we may need to be a bit kind to ourselves in that time too.

'Take just two breaths this time. Not even three. I'll show it to you and then I'll let you try it. Step one, as you breathe in, you silently tell yourself, "I do my best!" Then breathe out, "I let go of the rest!" That means, "I am doing my best. There are things that I cannot control. In business it could be raw material prices, exchange rates, etc. Breathing in, I do my best, breathing out, I let go of the rest."

'There is a saying.

If your compassion does not include yourself, it is not complete.

'So, many times, we think that compassion is only meant for other people. The fundamental thing is if you can't be kind to yourself, how can you be kind to somebody else? If you don't love yourself enough, how can you love somebody else enough? And if you don't take care of yourself, how are you going to take care of other people? So, compassion, like charity, begins at home. It starts with you.

What is completely available to you is the present moment, is now.
Now is in your hands, tomorrow is not.
By being in the present moment and doing what is required now, you start to construct your future.

'Pay full attention to the task at hand, instead of procrastinating. And with complete involvement start doing it. That is what shapes the future. By being more aware, more skilful in the moment, you shape the outcome in a much better way.'

Sid absorbed Krish's words, letting them settle slowly in his mind. He reflected on the simplicity of the Zen story—the profound wisdom in doing what is needed, without overthinking or resisting. It was as if Krish had lit a small candle in the darkness of Sid's mind, showing him a path he hadn't considered before.

Sid nodded, his voice thoughtful. 'So, what you're saying is, instead of battling my anxiety or trying to outrun it, I should focus on what I can do now. Not tomorrow, not next week, just this moment. And do it to the best of my ability, with a sense of kindness towards myself.'

Krish smiled, his calm demeanour radiating reassurance. 'Exactly, Sid. Anxiety actually thrives in the gap between now and the imagined future. But when you shift your focus to the present and engage fully in what needs to be done, that gap disappears. And with it, so does the anxiety.'

If it's out of your hands, let it out of your mind too.

'Breathing in, you do your best. Breathing out, you let go of the rest.'

As Sid considered Krish's words, he felt the weight of his worry ease slightly. He realized the power of reclaiming the ongoing moment, of shaping his future by being fully present in the now. He was beginning to slowly understand how self-compassion could help him be kinder and gentler with himself. For if he could not do that, how could he be kind and gentle to others?

'A lot of people find it difficult to go to sleep because of an over-worked, stressed mind. And that is not a good thing because just like the body needs rest, the mind also needs rest.

'If we don't sleep well, there is no rest for the mind. So the body is partially resting but the mind is still thinking in some form or the other, which means it doesn't rest at all. This is why you wake up tired, because both the body and the mind are not fully refreshed.'

By giving ourselves kindness and self-compassion while we go through the human experience, we can avoid destructive patterns of negative thinking, emotions and behaviours and truly embrace what it is to be human.

'Yes, I for sure, have struggled with sleep. I will try this next time,' said Sid. 'I understand the importance of being kind to myself,' he added, his tone reflective, 'but isn't there a danger of it turning into feeling sorry for myself? How do I avoid that trap while still practising self-compassion?'

Sid took a deep breath, letting his dilemma settle in the stillness of the garden. The idea of being fully present resonated with him, but the struggle to differentiate between self-compassion and self-pity lingered in his mind. Krish's expression softened as he prepared to clarify the subtle but critical difference.

'What is pity? Pity is feeling sorry. Feeling pity for somebody comes from feeling that the person is not in a good place. So we start feeling sorry for them. Self-pity is when you feel sorry for yourself because you think you are not in a good place. Compassion, on the other hand, is love and kindness. Both of them are very positive emotions, pity is not. It is a negative emotion. In fact, it is fascinating that even the parts of the brain that get activated when you feel pity are very different from the parts of the brain that gets activated

Day 3: Meeting the Ghosts of Self-Criticism

when you feel kindness, love or compassion. The key thing to remember in all of this: mindfulness brings awareness and that will show you if you are feeling pity or compassion.'

Sid processed Krish's explanation. 'So, what you're saying is that pity, whether for someone else or for myself, comes from a place of feeling sorry—a negative emotion. It's almost like we're putting someone, or ourselves, in a position of weakness. But compassion is entirely different. Compassion is rooted in love and kindness, which are empowering and uplifting emotions.'

He looked at Krish with a renewed sense of clarity. 'I guess with enough practise, we can train ourselves to notice when our self-compassion starts to drift into self-pity and steer it back to where it belongs.'

'Yes. With practice, you should be able to develop the ability to see that you are lapsing into pity instead of compassion.' Krish replied. 'Self-pity is not a great thing. You can stay in bed all day feeling so sorry for yourself and that is not healthy at all!

'Self-compassion on the other hand is a healthy emotion. With awareness and mindfulness, it can be powerful. So, first and foremost, we need to work on building that level of awareness. Then all these things start to gain more clarity for us on our journey.

'You can think about mindfulness till the cows come home and nothing much would have changed. The question is about making the shift from thinking to embodiment, right?' Krish concluded with what seemed like an invitation for Sid to explore these ideas a bit further.

Sid leaned back, his hands resting on the rough wooden bench as he absorbed Krish's words. He glanced around the garden, his eyes falling on a tiny sprout pushing through the soil near Krish's feet. It struck him how effortlessly the plant seemed to grow, reaching for the sunlight without overthinking its purpose or process.

'I think I get it,' Sid said slowly, his gaze still fixed on the sprout. 'Self-pity keeps us stuck, doesn't it? It's like standing still and letting weeds grow around us. But self-compassion feels more like nurturing a seed—being kind, watering it, giving it a chance to grow into something stronger. The difference is subtle, but it's huge.'

He turned to Krish, a flicker of determination in his eyes. 'You're right, though. Reading about it or thinking about it isn't enough. I've read so much about self-development and leadership, but I still find myself trapped in my thoughts. I need to actually do it—to practise—don't I?'

Krish smiled knowingly, sensing the shift in Sid's tone. 'Exactly,' he said, leaning forward slightly as if to emphasize his next point a bit more.

'Was it easy for you to learn to walk? Was it easy for you to learn to speak a language or play an instrument or a sport? Everything has a certain amount of practise involved and mindfulness is no different. You have to practise but the good news is that with practise, it 100 per cent becomes embodiment. That's the good news.

'The even better news is that practise does not necessarily entail going to the mountains and standing on one foot or sitting in a cave. You can do these little practices on a day-to-day basis, every moment, breathing in and breathing out, as an opportunity to practise mindfulness. You will begin to embody it in time. It will happen!'

A little while later, Krish left Sid alone with his reflections and realizations. Sid picked up a fallen leaf and traced its veins with his thumb, feeling the texture under his skin. The simplicity of the moment mirrored the clarity of Krish's words.

Self-compassion is not complacency; it's courage.

The phrase circled in his mind, peeling back layers of his own harsh judgments and the self-critical patterns he had carried for years.

The rays of the afternoon sun were casting a bright golden hue over the entire place. The occasional rustle of the leaves made for a soothing rhythm. There was something about the place that really spoke to Sid. *I wonder if I could ask Krish to let me stay longer.* Was he looking for certainty or was he sensing something beyond?

'Sure. Stay on for a few more days. You'll know when it's time to leave!' was Krish's response when Sid sought him out later in the afternoon with his request.

Back in his room that night, Sid placed the leaf in his journal as if to bookmark this turning point. He closed his eyes and took a few deep breaths. His senses picked up a few familiar scents and sounds. He sat at the table and looked at the tree in the distance. The bamboo leaves rustled as they whispered their secrets to Sid. Did he understand what they were saying?

He flipped to a blank page and let his thoughts flow.

Krish's words about negative thinking and self-compassion revealed a truth I'd ignored for far too long—I've often been my harshest critic. I have a choice to be my own ally.

I can keep feeding the negativity, or I can pause, breathe and let self-awareness guide me. I can be kind to myself—not out of pity, but out of respect for my own humanity.

Self-compassion isn't weakness. It's a quiet strength that allows me to fail without being defined by it, to rise without being burdened by fear. It's the light I can turn on in the darkness of self-doubt.

I know now that the same effort I put into achieving and pushing can be channelled into understanding and embracing myself. It's not about perfection; it's about presence.

> One breath at a time. One step at a time. That's how I'll move forward.
>
> Self-compassion includes mindfulness, knowing that you're not alone, kindness and cognitive reframing.
>
> **My little practice:** Breathing in, I do my best. Breathing out, I let go of the rest.

Sid closed the journal and leaned back on the simple wooden chair. The weight on his chest felt a little lighter, his thoughts a little clearer. Outside, the wind rustled more strongly through the trees, as if nature itself was applauding his newfound resolve.

Day 4: Emotions and the Human Condition

The woods felt alive. As Sid walked along a narrow path, he looked up occasionally at the towering trees. Their branches looked like arms cradling the sky. The air was fresh and a bit damp. It had with it the unmistakable scent of wildflowers. Patches of sunlight danced on the ground.

Earlier in the day, Krish had invited Sid to join him on a walk. 'I'm going to park the truck at a certain point and take a walk into the woods today. Would you like to come along? If we're lucky, we may get to see some interesting sights.'

Activity in the woods had a different quality. Leaves rustled in the wind. Birds chirped incessantly and an occasional small creature could be heard darting through the brush. And despite this liveliness, there was a deep stillness in the place that made Sid feel small.

Krish was ahead and Sid saw him slowly bending and crouching near a moss-covered log. He appeared to be studying something intently. As Sid approached, he saw a tiny stream of ants marching with purpose, carrying bits of leaves back to their nest. Krish motioned for Sid to sit beside him on the log.

Without looking up, Krish asked, 'What do you notice?'

Sid observed the ants for a moment; their tiny movements synchronized in a pattern he couldn't quite decipher. 'They're . . . busy,' he said finally. 'Always moving, always working. It's like they have no time to stop.'

Krish smiled and leaned back, letting the sunlight dapple his face through the branches. 'That's how many of us live our lives. Constant motion, driven by unseen forces. But unlike the ants, we often don't know what we're carrying—or why.'

Sid shifted uncomfortably, thinking of his past hectic lifestyle. 'You mean the baggage we carry?'

'Exactly.' Krish replied before resuming his stroll through the trees, stopping every now and then to keenly observe something.

Emotional baggage is the heaviest thing we carry around.

He paused, crouching again, this time to examine a cluster of bright red mushrooms sprouting from the base of an old tree. He gently traced their delicate edges with his fingers, as if greeting an old friend. 'Nature holds so many secrets,' he said, his voice barely above a whisper. 'Every sight has a story if we care to look closely.'

Sid stepped closer, intrigued by the vibrant fungi. 'You seem to notice things that most people would walk past,' he remarked.

Krish chuckled softly, straightening up and brushing dirt from his hands.

Noticing is the first step to understanding. Whether it's the patterns in the forest or the patterns in our minds.

As they continued walking, the forest opened to reveal a small clearing bathed in sunlight. The grass looked like it was scattered with diamonds as the dew glistened in the sunlight. A butterfly lazily flitted from flower to flower. Krish stopped again, turning to Sid. 'Here we are, the perfect spot to rest for a moment.'

They sat on a flat rock, its surface warm under the sun. Sid's eyes followed the butterfly's journey. A question had been forming in his mind ever since Krish had pointed out the ants. He finally decided to voice it.

'Krish,' Sid began, hesitating as he searched for the right words. 'We use the word "emotions" so much in our daily lives. I feel them all the time—stress, excitement, regret—but . . . what exactly are emotions?'

Krish's face lit up with a knowing smile, as though he had been waiting for this question. He leaned back on his hands, his gaze scanning the treetops. 'Ah, emotions. That's a question worth exploring.'

The forest seemed to hold its breath as Krish prepared to unravel the mysteries of emotions, its natural stillness a fitting backdrop for the conversation ahead.

Day 4: Emotions and the Human Condition

'But let me ask you first, what do you think are emotions?' said Krish.

'Are they . . . feelings?' replied Sid a bit tentatively.

'Okay, but what are feelings? Are they different from thoughts?' probed Krish further.

'We have so many thoughts. Are all of them emotions? How do we differentiate emotions from thoughts?'

'It's worth considering these aspects because although we use this word so frequently and we are highly emotional beings, we don't understand how the whole thing works.

'EMOTION, the word itself comes from Latin where "E" denotes "out" and "movere" is move. So, emotion is something that moves out. It's a thought that moves outward. It could be a thought that moves us too!

'We have about 70,000 thoughts in a day and there are 86,400 seconds in twenty-four hours. Now, if you take away the time that you are sleeping, when your brain is hopefully at rest, what are you left with? More than a thought per second. However, not all these thoughts become emotions.

'If you are thinking good thoughts about me right now, some of them might get converted into a positive feeling. If you are thinking negative thoughts, some of that might get converted into negative ones.'

Saying this, Krish paused. Sid stretched his legs out, leaning back against a tree trunk as a playful breeze rustled the leaves above. Patches of sunlight danced on the ground in response. Krish's words swirled around in his mind.

'So, if I understand this right,' Sid began, 'thoughts are like seeds scattering in the wind. They're always bursting forth from a tree. But not all of them land and grow into something. Emotions are like the plants that emerge when a seed takes root and grows outward. Positive thoughts can help us bloom while negative ones can make us feel heavy. And we have so many thoughts . . . more than one for every second we're awake. No wonder it's hard to keep track of them all.'

Krish nodded with a gentle smile, waiting for Sid to connect the dots.

'Does that explain why we feel so overwhelmed sometimes?' Sid continued, 'But it also makes me wonder—how do we even begin to notice what's happening inside us? How do we figure out which thoughts turn into emotions and why some slip by unnoticed?'

Krish turned and gestured to a sapling nearby, its tender leaves trembling in the breeze. 'You're asking the right questions, Sid. To understand emotions, we first need to develop awareness—like noticing this young tree among the towering ones around it. Awareness happens in stages and it begins earlier in life than you might think.'

As Krish began to explain, Sid found himself leaning in and listening deeply.

'Understanding emotions needs awareness. When we are born, the first thing we become aware of is our body. As babies, we initially don't even know that we are separate from our mothers. We think we are a part of our mother. After some time, we develop an awareness of our own bodies. Slowly, we start to recognize ourselves in the mirror.

'Then follows a recognition of thoughts. We then become aware of our mind. We learn that we can think and feel.

'Even as adults, we are more aware of our body because it's physical and tangible, because we can touch it. We are a little less aware of our thoughts, because there are so many of them. While we can be aware of some common emotions, a lot of underlying emotions are hard to comprehend. They operate under the radar, so to speak. So, how do we develop a greater awareness of these emotions and why do we need to? Intuitively, we all understand that we need to manage our emotions. But doing so is tricky.

> Once, there was a man sitting on a park bench with a baby. There were other babies and young mothers in the park, all playing. After a while the baby started crying. The man tried pacifying him but nothing worked. The baby cried even louder.
>
> The man was very calm, though. He just kept repeating, 'It's okay Albert, it's okay Albert, calm down Albert.' The baby went on crying. A mother passing heard this and offered to help. She looked at the baby and asked, 'Why is little Albert crying?'
>
> The man looked at her and replied, 'I am Albert. He is Robert.'

'That was Albert's way of managing his emotions in that moment,' Krish laughed.

Both men were silent for a few minutes. It seemed like even the woods were becoming aware of their emotions.

Sid broke the silence. 'That story about Albert managing his emotions reminded me of a time when I completely lost my cool.' He crouched down, picking up a twig and tracing idle patterns in the dirt.

Krish, leaning against a tree, folded his arms and tilted his head. 'Tell me about it,' he said, his voice calm and inviting.

Sid exhaled deeply, twirling a twig in his fingers. 'It was a couple of years ago, during one of the most high-stakes projects of my career. My team and I were working on a presentation for a major client—one of those deals that could make or break reputations. I'd assigned a diligent team member to present some critical projections. She was usually very reliable, so I didn't double-check her work.'

He paused, throwing the twig aside. 'During the presentation, the client flagged an error in the data. I could feel the room shift—the disappointment, the judgment. My chest tightened and I lashed out at my colleague right there, cutting her off sharply. After the meeting, I tore into her in front of the team.'

Sid kicked at a stone, the motion quick and agitated. 'I could see the hurt on her face. I knew the moment I snapped that I'd gone too far. But my frustration wouldn't let me stop. Later, I found out that the error wasn't even entirely her fault—it was a miscommunication between two departments. The guilt ate at me for weeks.'

Krish's expression didn't change, but his voice was softer when he spoke. 'And how did you handle things afterward?'

'I apologized to her privately the next day,' Sid said, rubbing the back of his neck. 'But the damage was already done. She was professional about it, but I knew I'd broken something—a trust that took months to rebuild. The worst part was how it affected the whole team's morale.'

Krish nodded thoughtfully, letting the silence settle between them for a moment. The rustle of the leaves seemed to mirror the swirling thoughts in Sid's mind.

'Sid,' Krish began, leaning forward slightly, 'your story is a powerful example of how emotions, when unchecked, can ripple out and affect everything around us. You've taken the first step by acknowledging what happened. The next step is learning to respond, not react.'

Sid looked up at him, his curiosity evident. The woods around them felt alive, a fitting yet unlikely backdrop for a lesson in emotional awareness.

Krish gestured toward the trail ahead. 'Shall we keep walking and talking?

> **Emotions are an essential part of being human but managing them skilfully is what sets great leaders apart.**
> **Being human means that we experience life emotionally!**

'There are probably as many theories about emotions as there are emotions themselves. And that is fine because human emotions are often examined from the perspective of art, poetry, philosophy, psychology, neuroscience, culture, etc. Theories say there are 7–8 primary emotions and around 10–12 others. But more than anything, I think it's the large range of experiences we can have that stem from these emotions that makes life incredibly rich.

'Many years ago, when I was in my late teens and even early twenties, I was not very good at recognizing or managing my emotions. People don't believe it today when I tell them that I used to have a bad temper. I used to get angry very quickly. Today they look at me and say, "Oh really? You don't look like that at all, you look very calm."

'It has been hard work and I have learnt to become aware of my emotions and manage them. As I progressed in my career, I realized that it was really crucial. Emotional intelligence is way more important than IQ. I started looking at my practice of mindfulness to help me make those corrections and become more emotionally aware and emotionally intelligent.'

Krish paused at looked up at the trees. It felt like he was taking a moment to acknowledge his life.

He then continued. 'Only when you are aware of your emotions can you manage them well. Everything else comes second. Take technical knowledge, for example. If you don't know something, you can find out. You can get other people to help you. But if you are not able to manage your emotions skilfully, it's difficult to be a good leader. Even when you think of leaders you admire and examine which qualities they have, you will see that emotional management is usually right up there.

'If we didn't have emotions, we wouldn't have music, poetry or art. Life would be pretty dry. We can agree that emotions are certainly useful, but we also think that we are extremely rational beings, don't we? Especially when it comes to decision-making.

'Nothing can be further from the truth.

'We are highly irrational and emotional beings. "Which job should I take?", "Should I marry this person or that person?", "Should I marry at all or not?"—these are questions a lot of people grapple with. All of them are based on emotions. All our big life decisions hinge on emotions.

'Even the decisions we take at work every day are based on emotions at an underlying level. If someone has had a bad day, had a fight with their partner, or you know they are feeling upset about something, do you think they would make high-quality decisions?

'They might like to think, "Oh, nothing affects me" but that's not true. Emotions do leak into our decision-making, whether we are consciously aware of it or not. So, how do we become aware of our emotions? There are fewer emotions than thoughts. So, hopefully, it is a little easier to become aware of them.'

Sid paused, looking around the woods as a gentle breeze rustled the leaves overhead. The sunlight danced on the ground, shifting like fleeting emotions themselves. 'It's strange, Krish,' he said. 'Out here in nature, everything feels so in sync. But with emotions, it's like we're always out of balance. How do we even begin to understand them?'

Krish gestured to the play of light and shadow filtering through the trees. 'Much like these patterns of light, emotions leave traces—sometimes subtle, sometimes bold. Let me share something fascinating that might help us notice them more clearly.

'Think about this. What happened the last time you were angry? Were you breathing short, small breaths? Was your face hot? What about the fingers, chest, arms? Anger manifests itself in a certain part of the body.'

'Oh yes!' said Sid. 'My face and ears become hot. I breathe short and fast. Sometimes my hands shake. Why, sometimes I even feel like punching someone!'

'Now, how do you feel when happy?' continued Krish.

'Hmmm. I think I feel light. A certain kind of aliveness in my whole body,' responded Sid.

'Exactly. A study in Finland (Nummenmaa et al., 2013) asked people how they felt when they experienced an emotion. They were given a sheet with a silhouette of the human body on it and asked to colour the place where that emotion was being felt. Interestingly, when researchers mapped those responses, they found that we humans experience emotions exactly the same way irrespective of gender or colour!

'People coloured "happy" in warm colours of red and orange throughout the body. They coloured anger as increased activation in the chest and face. They coloured depression in blue to convey reduced activation or dullness. This study and all other examinations of emotions show that emotions are nothing but thoughts manifesting in the body. To think of emotions in this way is to get a better grip on them.'

'Wow! This is fascinating! So if I become aware of what is happening in my body, I could get an insight into my emotions?' exclaimed Sid, excited at his discovery.

'Yes. Interestingly, we think that it's only the mind that is capable of thinking. That is not true. The brain has billions of neurons, but did you know the heart and the gut have thousands of them too? And they are constantly sending information up to your brain.'

'Amazing! Now I understand how we have "gut feelings",' said Sid. He was absorbing these insights and something told him that what he was learning had the power to change his life.

'Yes, information does not always only come from the brain. The neurons in the heart and the gut also produce information for us. Imagine how valuable it would be if we could learn to access that information,' Krish continued. He crouched down and picked up a small stone from the ground, tossing it lightly in his hand as if weighing its significance. 'Sid,' he said, his tone reflective, 'the body often knows things long before the mind catches up. It's like this stone—small, unassuming, but carrying a weight you can feel if you pay attention.'

He stood and turned to face Sid, tossing the stone into a nearby stream where it created gentle ripples. 'Let me tell you a fascinating experiment that shows just how much our body can tell us—if we're willing to listen.'

'In a study (Bechara et al., 1997), people were seated at a long table with four stacks of playing cards on it. Two stacks were red and two were blue. The stacks were kept face down and all people were told was to pick a card.

'Every time they picked a card, they would either win or lose points. They could see that on a screen but they were not told which cards were good or which stacks were good. They had to pick cards and figure it out by looking at the score.

'Now, here is what happened. Initially, it all looked random. Once people picked about fifty cards, they started to form a hunch. They got the sense that maybe the red stacks had good cards and the blue stacks didn't.

'After eighty cards, they figured it out. Their mind said, "Look, most blue stack cards are losing points. The red stack cards are good."

'So, the participants had a hunch at fifty cards and clarity after eighty cards.

'Now here is the fascinating next step. Researchers then hooked people up to a polygraph, a lie detector. They put wires on people's palms and measured their pulse rate. They started observing the polygraph as the game was played. At the tenth card, when the person's hand went towards the blue card, the body started sweating. The pulse went up a bit. The body was saying, "Don't pick that card."

'This has happened to us all at some point or the other, when you meet somebody and get a gut feeling about that person. Maybe at an interview or even a social meeting.

'Sometimes you are walking and your instinct tells you that you are being followed or that you should turn to look behind. Your gut tells you not to go a certain way when you are a bit lost and you come to a turning. It's happened to all of us. What do you think is happening?'

The body has a level of intelligence that is even beyond the mind. It knows things that even the mind doesn't know. Are you able to listen to it?

Sid rubbed his chin thoughtfully, replaying Krish's words in his mind. He leaned forward, resting his elbows on his knees. 'So, our body knows before our mind does,' he said quietly, as if testing the idea aloud.

Krish nodded, a glimmer of encouragement in his eyes. 'Exactly, Sid. Emotions have wisdom and the body conveys it in a language of its own. The question is—are we paying attention and listening to it?'

'We often say, "I am angry." Now, here is a question. If emotions are nothing but thoughts being experienced in the body, why do we say, "I am angry"? Why do we connect ourselves to the emotions so much that we become the emotion?

'Let me phrase that another way. If you have a headache, would you say, "I have a headache", or "I am a headache"? If you have pain in the neck, would you say, "I am experiencing pain in my neck" or say, "I am a pain in the neck"?

'If emotions are just being experienced in the body, why do we become the emotion? We, at some level, understand that we are not our thoughts. We also understand, at some level, that we are not our emotions. Yet, we identify with them so completely.

Day 4: Emotions and the Human Condition

'This is the trap that we fall into from a young age when we first start identifying with the body. The child says "me" and pats the body. If you live in a house, you don't say, "I am the house"; you simply live there. Likewise, we must understand that we are not our thoughts. I am thinking, these are the thoughts that are going on in my mind but that doesn't mean I am the thought, isn't it? Imagine for a minute if you were to believe and behave according to each of your 70,000 thoughts, what would happen?

'One minute you may be smiling at a person and the next minute you may feel inclined to tell them to shut up. You cannot behave according to every thought. Similarly, you cannot behave according to every emotion. Instead of saying, "I am angry", say "I am experiencing anger".

'When you listen to your body, it's telling you that there is anger going on right now. Your fingers are perhaps clenching into a fist. Shifting from the existential to the experiential is the key. It creates a little gap between you and the emotion. And in just making this shift in perspective, we already start to become more aware of our emotions. Thereby, we become better at managing them.'

You are not the body.
You are not the mind.
You are not the emotion.
You are merely experiencing all these things.

Sid sat quietly, staring at the ground where a small beetle was making its slow journey across the dirt. Krish's words echoed in his mind: *Shifting from existential to experiential.*

The idea felt both liberating and overwhelming. He flexed his fingers, noticing how even that small movement felt more intentional now.

Finally, breaking the silence, Sid looked up at Krish with a thoughtful expression. 'This sounds so profound. I'm sure it can be really powerful to have that degree of emotional control,' he said and asked eagerly 'So what should I actually do?'

'Hahaha. I love your enthusiasm,' laughed Krish. 'But everything in its time, my friend! For now, let us complete this experience of the woods and create the space for all your reflections and realizations to settle into your mind.' With that, Krish got up and dusted his jeans.

The afternoon deepened as Krish and Sid continued their walk. The woods seemed quieter now, as if mirroring the introspection both men carried. The steady crunching of their footsteps on the leaf-strewn path, the occasional rustle of a small animal going about its life and the call of the odd bird had a slower rhythm compared to the busyness earlier in the day.

When they eventually emerged from the woods, the sight of Krish's pickup parked under a massive banyan tree brought a sense of grounding. Sid paused to take one last look at the treetops swaying gently in the breeze. Krish, with his ever-present calm demeanour, opened the door to the truck and gestured for Sid to hop in. The drive back to the farm was quiet. The truck rumbled across the serene landscape through fields bathed in the glow of the sun. The silence in the vehicle hinted at reflections unspoken.

When the farmhouse came into view, its weathered walls glowing faintly in the light, Krish finally spoke. 'Take a break to settle into your thoughts, Sid. Sometimes, clarity comes in the spaces between conversations.'

Sid nodded, his mind still turning over Krish's words as he stepped out of the truck. He lingered for a moment, watching the shadows dancing on the ground before heading inside.

Sid spent the afternoon walking around and sitting under trees before heading back to his room. He continued reflecting on Krish's words.

The farmhouse had become quiet as the evening emerged. The gentle hum of crickets filled the air when Sid stepped outside, drawn by the soft glow of lanterns hanging from the porch. The sky stretched above him, a vast canopy of stars twinkling brightly against the inky darkness. The cool breeze carried with it the faint scent of jasmine, mingling with the earthy aroma of the surrounding fields.

He spotted Krish sitting on the porch, a cup of tea in hand. He was swaying back and forth, his posture relaxed yet attentive, almost as if he had been expecting Sid.

'Good evening, Krish! I've been thinking a lot about my emotions. I can see now how powerful they are and I can't wait to learn how I can gain greater control over them,' said Sid eagerly.

'Sure thing. Why don't you tell me the most frequent emotion you have that you'd like to learn control over?' asked Krish smilingly. He was really impressed with Sid's eagerness to learn.

'Oh. That's an easy one! It's my anger,' said Sid without any hesitation.

'Okay then. Let's see,' said Krish as he paused and closed his eyes.

Sid often saw Krish do this before responding. It seemed to him that by taking a few deep breaths, Krish was tapping into some inner reservoir of wisdom.

'Did your parents ever teach you to count to ten when you are angry?' Krish said as he opened his eyes after a few deep breaths.

'Yes!' smiled Sid as he recalled his mother gently admonishing him for throwing a tantrum and asking him to slowly count backward from ten to one. Her memory always brought a gentle smile to Sid's face.

'What does the counting do?' asked Krish but the question seemed rhetorical.

'It is an action that forces you to stop. Think of it as the sacred pause,' Krish resumed. There is a quote often attributed to Viktor Frankl: "Between stimulus and response there is a space. In that space is our power to choose our response. In our response lies our growth and our freedom."'

Krish paused. For Sid, it felt like the universe had too. He silently repeated the lines he had just heard, letting the power of their meaning sink deeply into him.

'So, the next time somebody says or does something that upsets you, just stop. Do not react, do not say anything in the moment. Just stop. Most of the time, the moment somebody says or does something, there is a trigger. We react and things get out of control. It is all because we don't follow this one simple step,' Krish said after a few pregnant seconds.

'I see what you mean. I can think of a million times when I've reacted, only to regret it a minute later! I have sent text messages and emails in reaction and a minute later scrambled to delete or undo them only to realize it was too late!' Sid remarked rather regretfully.

Day 4: Emotions and the Human Condition

'The next step is to take a breath with total awareness. The breath is the most powerful yet underused tool you have. It is the first thing you do when you are born and cry. It is the last thing you do as you leave this world. And yet, in between, it is quite completely unused!' said Krish with a little laugh. 'You will always have your breath with you. From the moment you are born till the moment you pass on.

'Tell me this, Sid, how do you breathe when you are experiencing anger?' Krish asked, this time looking directly at Sid so he knew a response was expected.

'My breathing is faster. I feel like it's also shallow, as if from the chest,' said Sid as he thought back to a time when he had been furious.

'Correct. Now tell me how you breathe when you are deeply relaxed,' continued Krish.

'Hmmm. I think I breathe a lot more slowly and deeply. In fact, if I think of someone who is sleeping, I realize now that the breath is even slower and deeper,' remarked Sid.

'The correlation is very simple, the breath changes with the mood or with the emotion. But you can also change the emotion by changing the breath. That is the secret.'

Every emotion is connected with the breath.
If you can change the breath, change the rhythm, you
can change the emotion.

Sid felt like he'd been hit by a bolt of lightning.

'So if I stop and take in five to ten deep breaths, I have stopped myself from reacting!' he said with excitement building in his voice.

'Exactly! You are a quick learner. By stopping and taking your awareness to your breath, you are gaining mastery over your emotion. The breath is the invisible thread that binds your body and your mind. By regulating it, you are regulating your emotions,' Krish summed up.

'The next step is to observe. Notice what your body is telling you. It will give you a message in that moment. Just observe. Listen. Is there any information coming from your gut, perhaps an indication why you are feeling the way you are? Remember how people in the study could tell which pack of cards was better?

'Emotions are complicated. People may react the same way to different emotions. For example, people shout in anger, guilt as well as shame. Many of these emotions can be bundled into categories. Therefore, it is important to observe the body because guilt will manifest itself differently from anger. The body will not lie about that. The mind, it will lie to you; it will tell you that it is the other person's fault, most of the time. But the body will tell you something a little truer. So pay close attention.' Krish paused again to give Sid space to reflect.

Sid's gaze shifted to the ground, his mind wandering to a moment he'd tried hard to forget. The air seemed to grow heavier as he delved into the memory of a long-ago argument with his former girlfriend, Aditi.

It had been a rainy evening and they were sitting in her apartment, the sound of raindrops against the windowpane doing little to diffuse the tension in the room. They had been discussing his tendency to overcommit to work at the expense of their relationship—a topic that had come up more than once. Aditi had said something that struck a nerve, though he couldn't admit it at the time.

'You know, Sid,' she had said, her tone calm but firm, 'you're amazing at solving other people's problems, but you're pretty terrible at dealing with your own.'

Her words cut deeper than she likely intended. Sid had always prided himself on being dependable, the one everyone could count on. But hearing her articulate something he secretly feared about himself—his avoidance of his own issues—felt like a slap in the face.

He lashed out instantly, his voice rising defensively. 'That's not true! You don't understand how much pressure I'm under. I'm juggling so many things—you think it's easy?' His words had come out harsher than he meant, but he was too caught up in the surge of emotions to stop.

Aditi had looked at him, her eyes filled with a mixture of frustration and sadness. 'Sid, I'm not trying to attack you. I'm just saying what I see.'

He could see now that her measured tone had fuelled his guilt, which had quickly twisted into anger. 'Well, maybe you should look in the mirror before pointing fingers at me!' he snapped, immediately regretting it.

In the days that followed, he had replayed the argument over and over in his mind. He knew she wasn't wrong—her observation had hit too close to home. The guilt of his reaction lingered like a dark cloud and when they eventually parted ways, he couldn't shake the feeling that he had damaged something irreparably that day.

As Sid came back to the present, he realized his fists were clenched and his chest felt tight. The memory still stirred a mix of guilt and shame within him. Looking at Krish, who waited patiently for him to process his thoughts, Sid took a deep breath, releasing the tension that had accumulated in his body.

'There was this one time I really wish I had stopped myself,' Sid said, his voice tinged with regret. 'She wasn't wrong and I lashed out at her because I couldn't handle hearing the truth.'

Krish smiled gently. 'The past can be a great teacher, Sid. Each memory like this gives you another chance to learn, to grow. With what you're discovering now, you can create a different future.

'Let's go to the final piece, Sid. As you observe, you may reflect with a calm mind on why the situation has unfolded a certain way. Why are you feeling like this? Most times, people are not bad and they are not trying to say or do something just for the sake of hurting you, upsetting you or making you angry. Are you feeling this way because of something that happened to you earlier? Are you carrying some baggage about this person? Is that why this is becoming a trigger now? After reflecting upon all this, you may choose to respond.

'Ask yourself a simple question—what is the response which will bring about the most favourable outcome in any situation? Often, you will realize that reacting is going to be counterproductive. By responding wisely, you can actually influence the outcome.'

'STOP! It's all coming together for me!' Sid suddenly shouted with excitement. His sharp mind had managed to see this as a step-by-step process. Krish smiled with amusement.

'I think I have the formula!' exclaimed Sid. 'When I'm triggered next, I know what I'm going to do. I'm going to

STOP and I mean that as an acronym,' he said, allowing himself a moment of pride for what he had made up.

'Tell me more,' encouraged Krish.

'The STOP practice. The S stands for "Stop", the sacred pause as you described it. The T stands for "Take a breath", the deep breathing with awareness to change the emotion. The O stands for "Observe" as I check in with my body to take stock of what information it has for me. Finally, the P is for "Proceed" as I choose the response that will get me the best possible outcome!'

'That's quite clever!' Krish remarked with a clap. 'It sounds like a simple and powerful way to remember the steps involved when you are triggered. Let's try this to understand it better.'

Sid nodded enthusiastically. He couldn't wait to see how this was going to unfold.

Krish stood up, stretching his arms toward the sky as if shaking off the weight of the conversation. 'Alright, my friend,' he said, looking down at Sid with a grin, 'If you're ready to put your STOP technique to the test, let's dive right into it.'

Sid rose eagerly, brushing the dust off his jeans. 'I've never been more ready. Let's do this.'

Krish motioned Sid to follow him and started to walk toward the lotus pond. They reached the wooden bench by the side of the pond. The stillness of the space felt perfect for the exercise ahead. When they reached the bench, Krish asked Sid to take a seat. 'Find a comfortable way to sit, Sid. This is a practice you can do anywhere, but it helps to begin in a calm and safe space.'

Sid nodded, adjusting his posture on the bench. The cool wood beneath him was grounding and the soft breeze that swayed the neem leaves above felt calming. He closed his eyes for a moment, letting the ambiance settle into his senses.

Krish took his place on a nearby patch of grass, crossing his legs as he observed Sid with quiet encouragement. 'This practice isn't about perfection, Sid. It's about curiosity and learning. Ready to begin?'

Sid opened his eyes briefly, nodding with determination. 'Absolutely.'

'Good,' Krish said, his tone lower and more focused. 'Close your eyes if you're comfortable,' he began, a gentle smile tugging at his lips. 'I'll guide you through the steps.' His deep voice was now like a magnet and Sid leaned back against the bench.

'First, recall an incident that made you really angry. Visualize it in your mind in as much detail as possible. Think about the situation, the circumstances and who was present. Picture their faces, clothes and actions.' Krish paused for a bit before resuming, 'Remember what was said.'

Sid vividly recalled the conference room filled with the hum of a high-stakes meeting. It had been one of those days when the pressure was palpable. Sid had spent weeks working on the presentation for a complex project involving his team. The management's buy-in was critical for the project's success and Sid had been eager to impress.

'What did that person say or do that made you angry or upset? What kind of words did they use? What were their actions like? And as you do that, bring out the emotions as well. How did you feel? Try to relive that emotion. Remember what you said, how you felt. Play it out in your mind like a movie.' Krish paused again.

Day 4: Emotions and the Human Condition

Sid cast his mind back into the past. He had been presenting and everything seemed to be going well until Rajiv, a colleague known for his brusque demeanour, had interjected. 'Sid, these timelines look unrealistic,' Rajiv had said, leaning back in his chair with what looked like a dismissive smirk. 'Have you even considered the operational constraints?'

Sid had frozen for a moment, feeling the weight of Rajiv's words and what he thought were judgmental glances from the higher-ups. Rajiv had continued, his tone seemingly dripping with condescension, 'This looks like a basic mistake.'

Sid had felt his chest tighten and heat rising to his face. It wasn't just Rajiv's words; it was the way he said them, in front of everyone, undermining Sid's credibility. The frustration and anger suddenly boiled over and Sid had lashed out. 'Maybe if you were more involved, you'd actually know the details,' he'd snapped.

The room had fallen silent, the tension thick. Rajiv had raised his eyebrows but not said anything more. The meeting had limped to its conclusion, but Sid's outburst had lingered, creating a palpable awkwardness with Rajiv for long after.

As Sid vividly recalled, he felt anger rising in him yet again. It was many months since the incident. And yet, it still angered him.

'Now, press pause in your mind and stop the movie,' Krish interjected.

'Take your attention to your breath. Is it short and quick or long and slow? Take your attention to your body. Can you notice where you might be experiencing the emotion? Is it in the face, or the chest, neck, hands, stomach?'

As Sid took note of his breathing, he realized that it was constricted and quick. He then observed he had involuntarily clenched his fists and his face was flushed.

'Now, let's play the movie again from the beginning. Recall what that person said or did and this time also reflect, gently asking the question, "Why did this person say or do what they did?"

'Perhaps because they wanted to bring about a certain outcome which they believed in. They thought it was going to be a positive outcome. Now, silently in your mind, form a response. Form the kindest, most positive response that you can think of. What kind of a response would have brought about a positive outcome?' Krish paused again for Sid to reflect.

As his body and mind calmed, Sid realized his reaction that day had been driven not just by anger but by a deeper sense of guilt and shame. He had overlooked a minor but critical detail in the timeline, one Rajiv had caught. Though Rajiv's delivery was harsh, his point was valid. Sid's guilt at having missed the detail had fuelled his defensive and aggressive response. He reflected on Rajiv's possible motivations. Why had Rajiv spoken the way he did? Slowly, he began to see the situation from another perspective.

Rajiv wasn't trying to undermine me personally, Sid thought. He was probably concerned about the project's feasibility and wanted to ensure we weren't setting ourselves up for failure in front of the clients. His delivery may have been harsh, but perhaps he felt the urgency to address a gap before it became a bigger issue.

The realization was bittersweet—he couldn't change the past, but he could take this learning forward. He saw clearly

Day 4: Emotions and the Human Condition

now how much power there was in choosing to pause, breathe and observe.

'Now, one last time, let's play the video out in your mind, but this time just when you come to the point in the visualization where you got upset or angry, introduce the kind response you just came up with and then let the scene continue. If this had been your response, what would that person have said or done? Would it be different? If so, how?' Krish's voice trailed off.

Sid rewound the memory to the exact moment when Rajiv had interjected during the meeting, his tone sharp and accusing. But this time, in his mind, instead of reacting defensively and letting his frustration dictate his response, Sid visualized a different scenario.

This time, he saw himself pausing. He imagined taking a deep breath, feeling the tension in his shoulders ease slightly. In his mind, he looked directly at Rajiv, his expression calm and open.

'Rajiv,' he imagined himself saying, 'I understand your concern and it's valid. Let's address it together. Perhaps we can go over the specifics after this meeting and ensure we're covering all the bases.'

In this reimagined scenario, the room didn't feel heavy with tension. Rajiv's furrowed brow softened and he nodded, acknowledging Sid's response. 'That makes sense,' Rajiv said in this scenario, his voice calmer. 'Let's do that.'

Tears were flowing down Sid's face but he made no attempt to hide them or to wipe them away. They were tears of catharsis. Sid continued to play the scene in his mind. The higher-ups, who had been observing, appeared reassured. The focus shifted back to the project and the meeting moved forward productively. There was no lingering awkwardness, no undercurrent of conflict, just a constructive, respectful exchange.

It's amazing how different it could have been, Sid thought. *If only I had paused and chosen to respond with understanding instead of reacting emotionally.*

For the first time since the incident, Sid felt a sense of release. The weight of guilt he realized he had carried—of lashing out and damaging his relationship with Rajiv—felt lighter now. More importantly, he understood that he had the tools to approach such situations differently in the future. The power to change was in his hands and it started with a simple pause and a mindful response.

They sat in silence for almost the next half hour. Sid noticed that the lotus bud had bloomed a little more than it had on his first day. He felt that he could almost relate to the bud at that moment. He was also trying to rise above the muddy waters of his past.

Twilight had a magical quality that provided a canvas for Sid as his mind swirled with relief, clarity and also a strange sense of empowerment. The cool evening air enveloped them slowly.

Finally, Sid shifted slightly, breaking the silence. He hesitated for a moment before speaking, his voice thoughtful yet tinged with curiosity.

'Krish, I have a question for you. I certainly feel very calm now. I had a very different response as I followed your guidance today. In fact, it changed the outcome of the whole thing. But how am I going to do this in real time? I can't tell that person who is triggering me to wait so I can go breathe, reflect and come back!' Sid broke the silence eventually.

'Hahaha . . . what we did now is a simulation. It is practise,' Krish chuckled as if he was waiting for this question.

'What happens when you go to the gym? You lift weights to build muscles. You learn karate with a punching bag or with a partner, but come the day you get into a fight, you know how to do it. It's the same principle. This is a simulation. The more you do these simulations with past instances or past episodes, the more you change the wiring in your head. You make new connections in your brain and strengthen the new connection,' Krish explained

'Slowly, you will see what is happening, even before or as it happens. You will see your reaction emerge, your anger arising in the body. You will feel your chest get hot, but you will already be forming a much more emotionally intelligent response.

'The key here is practise.

'When you develop this capability of distinguishing that you are not the emotion, there is a gap that gets created between you and the emotion. And over time with considerable practise, the gap widens and you have absolute control over that gap to an extent where even your perspective of pain can be different.'

Your problem is not the problem. It's your reaction that's the problem!

'So basically, it's like strength training. The more I practise, the stronger my mental muscles become and then they do the heavy lifting required in the moment!' said Sid.

'Exactly.' Krish smiled at Sid. 'Let me share a story with you of how even a simple pause and breathe can reduce or even remove your suffering.

Years ago, my friend and I were riding across the countryside on a motorcycle. It was a Sunday morning. At one point, a dog dashed across the road. My friend, trying to avoid hitting the dog, lost control of the bike and we both landed in a ditch. My friend had a number of bruises. I had a bad cut on my knee. It was bleeding quite profusely.

We then picked ourselves up, somehow took the bike out of the ditch and made our way to a little village nearby. In that sleepy one horse town, there was only one doctor. And he was not a surgeon. He could clean up my friend's wounds with antiseptic, but he said that I would need stitches for the cut on my leg. There was just one small problem. He did not have anaesthesia. He had a needle and sutures, but no anaesthesia.

I figured it was better to stitch the wound than not, so I asked him to go ahead. He was unsure, saying that it would be very painful without the anaesthesia. But I insisted and assured him I would manage the pain. As he prepared the needle, I prepared myself with a number of deep breaths. He then proceeded to stitch me up. While he was stitching me up, I kept taking deep breaths and talking with my friend. At some point, the doctor said to me 'Are you okay? Here I am stitching you up and you are talking calmly to your friend. What is the matter? Are you not normal and do you not feel the pain?!'

So I responded to him and said, 'Yes, of course there is pain, but that's it. There is no suffering.'

Sid leaned forward, his face illuminated in the glow of dusk. He seemed captivated, almost incredulous, as Krish finished his story. After a moment of contemplation, he said, 'So you're telling me you actually felt the pain but didn't let it overwhelm you. You didn't spiral into thoughts like, "Why did this happen to me?" or "This is unbearable". You just accepted it as pain and stayed present with it.'

Sid paused, as though absorbing the depth of what he'd just said. 'It's fascinating. Pain is inevitable, but the suffering—that's something we add to it with our thoughts, isn't it? It's the stories we tell ourselves, the endless overthinking that turns pain into something far worse. That's what you avoided.'

He shook his head, a wry smile tugging at his lips. 'I can't imagine calmly talking to someone while being stitched up without anaesthesia. But I get it now—it's the separation between the pain and the narrative around it. That's the real power.'

Sid's voice softened, the realization settling in. 'It's like you found a way to keep the pain in its place without letting it take over your mind.'

Krish nodded approvingly, a gentle smile on his face. 'Animals feel the pain when they get injured, but they don't linger over it. By putting this distance between the emotion—between what is happening—even if it is at a physiological level, you give yourself a much better way of coping with it.

'I am not saying that the next time you face a physical injury, you should just behave as if nothing happened. No, that is not what mindfulness is all about. It just brings a greater degree of awareness and skill into the process. If you take the emotion out of pain, you needn't suffer. You can just feel the pain at a physical level and move on.

'This is not about avoiding, suppressing or denying. I will not say, "Oh, I am totally fine, I am not feeling bad at all", because bottling up is not healthy at all. It is about acknowledging, understanding and then being able to work with it and manage it, right? So, it is basically about reducing harm to ourselves and others. By being aware of our emotions, we can make much better decisions.

'So, working with these perspectives and learning how to manage your emotions can give you a much better ability to deal with people and situations. It will make you a better leader, a better person, while improving interpersonal and leadership skills.

'Remember, working with emotions is a lot like being a lotus flower. Grow in the muddy water, yet don't let the water touch you.'

Sid asked, 'Is anger always a bad emotion?'

'Anger is often thought of as a bad emotion, but I would say that's not necessarily true. What can become bad is the way anger manifests or the way anger is expressed. By itself, the emotion need not always be bad. For example, if there has been injustice and you feel anger in that moment, that would be perfectly alright and justified. What is important is how you express it and how to manifest it. If you were to get abusive and violent, it is bad. But you can also take that very powerful, very strong emotion and use it in amazing ways.

'For example, what did Mahatma Gandhi do? He was angry at the fact that we had been exploited by the British. But he took that anger and translated it into a non-violent movement. Anger can change the course of history, literally.

'It has to be looked at more closely but almost always an unaware expression of anger is bad. Awareness brought to the emotion makes you look at the emotion and why it is happening. Then come up with a wise way of responding, that's important.'

Negative emotions are a part of the human experience. Wanting a life without negative experiences is like wishing for only day and no night. The day doesn't exist without night. Just like there is no wrong without right. And there is no left without right.

The evening brought a soothing hush with it, as if to remind everyone that nature was winding down for the day. The crunch of leaves underfoot provided the perfect contrast.

As they reached the cottage, Sid turned to him with a thoughtful expression. 'Today has been . . . enlightening. I hadn't realized how much I needed this space to reflect.'

Krish nodded, a serene smile playing on his lips. 'It's a journey, Sid. Awareness takes practise, but every step counts. Our journeys through life always have lessons for those who listen.'

After a simple dinner, Sid retreated to his room, his mind buzzing with the day's insights. The soft light of the lamp illuminated the journal on his desk, its blank pages inviting him to capture his thoughts.

The cool evening breeze danced in through the window. The bamboo leaves rustled. In the distance the big tree seemed to wrap the day in its embrace so that night could come.

Sitting down, Sid began to write.

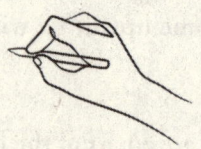

> Today was about noticing—both the world around me and the world within me.
>
> Emotions are thoughts that move outward.
>
> Emotions are not who we are; they are what we experience.
>
> Emotional intelligence is not about suppressing or ignoring emotions but pausing long enough to see them for what they are and then using that information to choose how to act.
>
> Awareness is the bridge between emotion and action.
>
> **My little practice:** I Stop. I breathe. I observe my body, mind and emotions. I consider before I respond.
>
> **Reflection question:** What are the emotions I frequently struggle to manage well?

Sid closed the journal with a sense of quiet resolve. The trees outside his window were bathed in moonlight, their stillness mirroring the calm he felt within. For the first time in a long while, he felt a flicker of hope that change was not only possible but already beginning.

Part 2

Leading Yourself: Building an Intentional Life

Day 5: Mindfulness: A Way of Life

The walls of the cottage shone with the golden light of the morning sun as it streamed in through the windows. Sid could smell the dew drenched grass in the crisp air as he stepped out onto the veranda and stretched. The birds were already chirping in their excitement at a new dawn. Four days had passed since Sid had come and the place was already feeling like home.

Krish was already there, seated at the weathered wooden table with two steaming mugs of tea as if he knew exactly when Sid was going to join him. He greeted Sid with a warm smile, his calm presence as grounding as the warm sunlight of the morning.

'Good morning, Sid,' Krish said, gesturing to the seat across from him. 'How are you feeling now after a few days of exploring mindfulness?'

Sid sat down, wrapping his hands around the warm mug and letting its aroma fill his senses. 'Morning, Krish. I feel . . . lighter, more alive than I have felt in ages. But I also feel like I'm just scratching the surface of something much bigger.'

Krish nodded with a smile. 'That's a good place to be—a mix of curiosity and openness. It means you're ready to dive deeper.' He took a sip of tea and leaned forward slightly, his voice lowering just enough to draw Sid in.

'"Intention, intensity and right action" is my simple formula for life,' he said.

'Everything that comes into existence begins when a thought becomes an intention. But intention alone is not enough. It will remain an intention unless it is fed with intensity. And the degree of intensity dictates how powerfully the intention manifests. If your intensity is weak, your intentions may take a long time to turn into action. On the other hand, if your intensity is strong, you will obsess over the intention and devote your entire being to make it come alive. And finally, remember that even with the intention and a high level of intensity, right action is necessary. Taking mindfulness to your actions leads to the right action.

'At some point of time, you will actually be able to watch your thoughts—the useful intentions will then be clearly visible to you. You then pick the intentions you want to feed. By watching yourself and responding with awareness, choosing the right actions to do, you will be able to transform your life.'

'So are you saying that I need to be aware of my intentions to pick the ones I want to feed and not waste my intensity feeding every intention?' asked Sid.

'Absolutely!' said Krish. 'Imagine this. You are standing on a railway platform. There are different trains coming and going. You will not jump onto each one, will you? You will wait for the right train you want to catch. The thoughts in your head are like these trains. You observe them but you do not want to run after each one of them. Just like you will stand by and let the wrong trains pass, you will observe your thoughts until you see the right thought. That is the one you pick as an intention and decide what degree of intensity it deserves. And then, just like the right train, it will take you to the right destination.'

'I think I get it now!' Sid exclaimed excitedly. He felt like the clouds had suddenly parted to reveal the bright shining sun.

'I may have an intention to make money. But with mindfulness, I can choose how much money is important to me. And then the awareness of the right action to manifest the intention dictates that I work hard to achieve that goal and not rob a bank.'

Krish chuckled. 'That is an interesting way of putting it.'

'But as I go about everyday life, how do I ensure that I constantly have the space and ability to do this? There are so many distractions that I'm worried my monkey mind will take me in the wrong directions,' said Sid

'True. Which is why you need to practise mindfulness as a way of life. Not merely as something you do on the mat or with your eyes closed for ten minutes a day.'

Mindfulness is not something you do. It is a state you are in, no matter what you do!

'Let me introduce you to a powerful mindfulness technique today—integrated practice. It is integrated with life, every moment, everything you do. The best part—you don't need time for an integrated practice. You don't have to sit somewhere. You don't have to close your eyes. Integrated practice is a way of doing things you are already doing, but doing them differently.'

Krish paused, letting his words settle. He leaned back slightly and looked at Sid with a calm yet focused expression. 'Let me explain this with a little wisdom from the Zen master, Thich Nhat Hanh,' he continued, his tone steady and inviting.

'He says, "Mindfulness is the energy of being aware and awake to the present moment. It is the continuous practice of touching life deeply in every moment of daily life. To be mindful is to be truly alive, present and at one with those around you and with what you are doing. We bring our body and mind into harmony while we wash the dishes, drive the car or take our morning shower."

'It is a beautiful and elaborate definition. When you add "ness" to a word, it becomes a noun. So happy becomes happiness, sad becomes sadness, lonely becomes loneliness. These are all different energy states. Likewise, mindful becomes mindfulness. And since a noun is a name or a place or a thing, we can conclude that mindfulness is a thing. Mindfulness is an energy! And when you are constantly generating this energy, it gives you exactly that quality of mind you need to go about everyday life with grace and wisdom. Every moment, wherever you are, is an opportunity to increase the energy of mindfulness.

'It is possible through these integrated practices to be mindful all the time. Imagine yourself as a mobile phone. You plug it in and you leave it to charge. At some point, it is fully charged. And then you start using it. Depending on your usage, the battery starts draining, till at some point, you decide to charge it again.

'Now, imagine if there was a way in which phones could be charged automatically by the air around them and didn't need to be plugged in anywhere. As human beings, if you think of mindfulness as an energy, you can constantly charge yourself with that energy.'

'Ah okay. I get it! A dedicated practice like the ones you guide me through is like plugging into a socket and getting charged. The "my little practice" that I have been making for myself every day is like plugging in for a few minutes every now and then to get a little bit of charge. What you are talking about now as integrated practice is an advanced technology. It allows you to keep charging yourself every moment without having to plug in anywhere!' said Sid.

Krish smiled knowingly, sensing Sid's eagerness. 'Yes. And that is why it is so powerful. If you practise integrated mindfulness, trust me, you can even go for days together without a dedicated practice.

'Let's start with one of my favourites—something most of us start the day with—brushing our teeth. Now think about this, when you go to brush your teeth, how long do you take typically? Most people say two minutes. I take ten. I take the brush and look at the bristles. I feel the texture of the bristles before I put paste on them. I observe the colour of the paste, smell it and then close my eyes. I sit down and I brush my teeth. I take about eight to ten minutes, depending on the day. Never less than eight minutes. When I brush, I can feel each bristle going into every part of my mouth.

'It's such a beautiful experience. You get the fragrance of the paste, the foaminess in your mouth and when you take some water and you gargle and spit, everything is so fresh. It's a way of bringing mindfulness to something as simple as brushing your teeth. The bonus—in all these years, I have never had any dental problems,' laughed Krish.

Sid nodded slowly, his curiosity growing. 'So, mindfulness isn't only about finding extra time or doing something entirely new,' he reflected. 'It's about turning the mundane into something meaningful by just being fully present in the moment.' He glanced at Krish, an amused smile forming. 'I never thought brushing my teeth could be an experience worth savouring.'

Krish chuckled. 'Exactly, Sid! When you bring your attention to even the smallest details, every activity becomes a portal to accessing the energy called mindfulness.'

Eager to understand more, Sid leaned forward. 'I guess that means this can go beyond brushing. It could be applied to . . . anything?'

Krish's face lit up. 'You can apply this technique to pretty much any activity. For example, how often do you pay attention while you are showering? While you step in there, splash some water, use some soap, you are probably busy planning the day, already having discussions with your colleagues in your head. Showering is a wonderful way of practising in-the-moment integrated mindfulness. Just notice the temperature of the water, take in the fragrance of the soap—every moment of that shower can become absolutely magical.'

Day 5: Mindfulness: A Way of Life

Krish paused, letting his words about mindful showering sink in.

Sid chuckled, shaking his head. 'You know, Krish, if I start taking magical showers and brushing my teeth for ten minutes, my family might think I've lost it.'

Krish laughed heartily. 'Well, tell them you're upgrading your life, Sid. After all, who doesn't want a more mindful family member?'

Sid grinned. 'Alright, showers and brushing—got it. But what about something less . . . wet? Surely mindfulness isn't just about what happens in the bathroom.'

'Of course not!' Krish replied with a twinkle in his eye. 'What about walking? It's something we all do—walking from one desk to another, walking to office, walking within the office, walking to the pantry, walking to the restroom, walking as an exercise. It is a wonderful way of practising mindfulness. Be aware of every movement and notice how beautiful it is to walk. It's an incredibly complicated activity that you are doing. As babies when we started walking, it took us all quite some time to learn it. Once we learnt it, we completely took it for granted.

'Any activity in this way can become an opportunity to practise mindfulness. It could be yoga or any exercise, talking with somebody, making a presentation. It could be writing out an email or making a phone call. All of these are opportunities to charge yourself up with energy.

'Just try doing this and in no time, you will see a difference. You will just start feeling lighter and happier. If you are practising mindfulness, that energy inside you is so amazing that you are always happy. You don't need an external reason to feel light or joyful.'

Krish paused, letting the gentle rustle of the leaves in the morning breeze fill the space between them. The sun was warmer now but softened by the canopy of trees above, casting dappled patterns on the ground. A faint birdsong added a melodic undertone to the tranquil scene.

Sid leaned back, soaking in the atmosphere, and said, 'You're right, Krish. It's like everything around us is already inviting us to be mindful—if only we pay attention.'

Krish smiled, gesturing toward the swaying branches. 'Exactly, Sid. And this presence can extend to how we interact with others too.

'Let's look at just one use case of this technique—mindful listening. It is a way of listening without judgement, criticism or interruption while being aware of internal thoughts and reactions that may get in the way of people communicating with you effectively. Now, in order to understand this better, let's look at how we usually listen to people.

'Normally when someone is speaking to us, our mind is somewhere else. We are probably looking at them and shaking our heads, not really listening. Or even if we are listening to them, in our heads, we are already preparing a reply. Or we are judging them, "Oh, what are you saying? What do you know? You just sound so stupid right now." All this chatter is going on inside. In fact, I would go to the extent of saying that today almost everyone has developed a listening disability. We can hear but we can't listen!

'Mindful listening is the practice of completely taking your attention to what is being said without the interference of the mind. It's a beautiful practice. It helps you understand what is being said, what is not being said and what is being felt in order to immediately establish a bond with the speaker.'

Day 5: Mindfulness: A Way of Life

As Krish paused, Sid's mind drifted to an incident. 'I remember, one morning, I was leaving for work and my girlfriend Aditi said, "Hey, can you come back on time or a little early in the evening? I want to make a special dinner today." So I said, "Yeah sure, I will do that."

'It was a busy day and that evening I got really tied up. I was in a meeting that ran a little late. I could not even text her saying, "Hey, I am running late." I finished up at work and I went home, I was about an hour or so late. When I rang the bell, she opened the door, just looked at me and went inside. I realized she was upset.

'I closed the door and said, "Hey, sorry, I am a little late." She said, "It's okay." So I thought, "Fine, everything is okay." I washed up and said, "Come, let's have dinner." I sensed something was not right. She was being rather cold towards me. I sat down and started eating, but she wasn't talking to me. After some time, I looked at her and said, "Hey, what's the matter, is something wrong?" She said, "Nothing." So again I didn't broach it further.

'After some time, she asked, "Do you know what day it is today?" So I said, "Yeah, it's Wednesday." She just looked back at me angrily.

'"What? It is Wednesday!" She just shook her head and went back to her food. We ate in silence for another two minutes. Then, she turned to me and said, "You don't love me anymore."

'I realize now that I had completely failed to listen. I had asked, "Is something wrong?" She had said, "No, nothing." But actually, everything was wrong. Nothing meant everything in that moment!'

'Yes. Sometimes people say something to you when they mean the exact opposite. You have to listen for what they are not saying, so you have to read between the lines. You have to understand how they are feeling.' Krish responded.

'When somebody speaks to you, give them your complete attention. Don't text, don't do anything else. Look at them, respectfully listen to them and you see how it changes their behaviour towards you. It will dramatically change your relationships,' Krish continued.

'This is in fact one of the most powerful and ignored lessons in leadership. If you want to be a great leader, whether at work or otherwise, develop the ability to listen. You will understand much more than what is being said. There are so many insights that can come to you that will allow for better decision-making and maintaining relationships. So just stop, listen for what is being said, listen for feelings and listen for what is left unsaid.'

Deep listening is the kind of listening that can help relieve the suffering of another person.

Sid sat back, a contemplative expression settling on his face. 'So, it's not just about hearing the words,' he began, piecing it together, 'but about understanding what lies behind them. When someone says "nothing" it could mean everything. When someone says, "You don't love me", it could mean they're in need of love. Listening isn't just about what's being spoken—it's about tuning into the unspoken, the emotions, the pauses, even the contradictions.'

He paused, nodding slightly as he processed further. 'I see how you mean that this isn't just about personal relationships. It's a skill I could use everywhere—work, friends, family. If

I can listen like this, truly listen, I'd probably solve half the misunderstandings before they even start. And in leadership, wow . . . if I could catch what's not being said in a meeting, I'd probably be miles ahead in decision-making and building trust.'

Krish smiled warmly, clearly pleased. 'Exactly, Sid. Listening is the simplest yet most underrated skill in life and leadership. And the best part? It's something we can start practising right now.'

Sid eagerly leaned forward. 'How do we do this, Krish? How do I practise listening like that?'

Krish stood up, stretching slightly before stepping into the cottage. He emerged a minute later holding a beautiful bowl and a small mallet, motioning Sid to follow him. 'Let's not just talk about it. Let's experience it. Come with me—we'll do a simple exercise.'

The two men walked toward a shaded grove where the rustling leaves created a serene ambiance, setting the stage for the lesson ahead.

'I am going to just ask you to sit and concentrate on the sound of my bowl. But before you do that, relax your body and mind. When we are relaxed, listening happens automatically.

'To start with, notice the way you are sitting. Observe tightness or tension in your body. Use your awareness to give yourself permission to relax. Notice your feet on the ground, notice the contact with the surface on which you are sitting. Take a couple of breaths to relax your body first. On the inhale, allow it to expand. On the exhale, allow it to relax. Let your mind settle. Breathe normally—simply notice that you are breathing. As you feel the sensation of a breath, notice how it is cool when you breathe in and warm when you breathe out. Notice the beginning of the inhale—how it goes in and how it ends. Notice the exhale—how it goes out and how it ends. Can you feel that there is one gap at the end of the inhale, before the exhale begins, and another at the end of the exhale, before the inhale begins. Just take your attention to your breaths and the gaps in between. Take your awareness now to your stomach, your belly. Notice how it rises and falls as you breathe. Gently place your hand on your stomach. Notice how when you breathe in, it expands, and when you breathe out, it contracts.

'There is nowhere else to be right now, nothing else to do, just being here and now. Take your complete awareness to the sound of the bowl.' Krish tapped the mallet against the bowl. The sound had a magical quality that reminded Sid of the temple bells he'd heard as a kid.

'Watch the sound as it rises and it slowly fades, staying alert, awake and aware, waiting for this sound to repeat.' Krish's voice was now even softer. He tapped the bowl again.

'Stay alert and as soon as the sound starts, let it fill your awareness. Listen to it without judgement or expectations till it completely fades.' The bowl sounded again.

'If you can hear other sounds, remain aware of those sounds as well, but focus on the bowl.' The bowl sounded. Deep yet gentle, the reverberations lingered in the air.

'Awareness of sound is just like eyesight. You can centre your attention on one thing but your peripheral vision also allows you to be aware of other things.'

The bowl kept sounding periodically as Krish's instructions continued as a melody.

'Stay alert like a cat waiting for a mouse. Take your awareness to your breath as you inhale and exhale. Observe the body now. Taking your awareness to the body, notice the sensation of touch, the contact with the ground. We will now close this practice with one deep inhale and exhale. Whenever you are ready, slowly and softly open your eyes.'

Well after the final echoes of the bowl had faded into stillness, Sid slowly opened his eyes, blinking as he reoriented himself to the present. The serene surroundings seemed to have suddenly taken on a new depth—he could see each leaf on the tree swaying gently, their colours more vivid, and the chirping of birds felt sharper, more distinct.

He shifted slightly in his seat, noticing the deep sense of calm that had come over him. He took a deep breath, feeling the rhythm of his body settle, and glanced at Krish, who was watching him with an encouraging smile. Sid couldn't help but smile back, a mix of awe and reflection in his expression.

'That was . . . interesting to say the least,' Sid murmured, his voice much softer than usual. 'I don't think I've ever paid that much attention to a single sound before.'

Krish leaned forward, his tone as gentle as the practice they had just completed. 'Good. Now, let's explore what happened during the practice.

'Was your mind wandering? What kind of mind wandering was it? Did you judge the sound of the bell? Did you start thinking about the other things on your mind? Was there an urge to move on? Did anything else happen for you? Were you able to pay complete attention to the sound?'

Sid smiled thoughtfully as he reflected: 'I did catch my mind wandering—thinking about lunch, of all things! And I noticed how quickly I judged the sound of the bowl the first time I heard it, almost wishing it would never end. But the moments I could fully focus, it felt really calming, like the sound filled the entire space in and around me.'

He looked at Krish, curiosity piqued. 'How else can I practise this? I can already see it's such a powerful way to train the mind.'

'This is a wonderful practice to build your ability to listen. But there are so many ways of doing this. You can just listen to any sound and build a practice. For example, at some point in my own practice, I would not pick up my mobile phone as soon as it rang. I chose a very pleasant tune for my ringtone, something that I really liked. Whenever it rang, I would let it ring for a couple of seconds. I would just take my awareness to the sound, notice it for a few seconds and then pick up. It can be any sound—don't judge a sound as good or bad. It's amazing that when you get deeply involved with the sound, your perspective of the sound will also shift.

'Many years ago, my office had pigeons that would sit outside the windows. The pigeons would make a cooing noise and my colleagues would get really upset listening to that noise. I asked why it bothered them. "Why don't you use it as a way of becoming more mindful?" I told them. They first thought I was crazy, but then we started to practise and I taught them for a couple of days. What happened next was amazing. The noise of the pigeons cooing did not bother people anymore. Instead they began to find it meditative. So, during a stressful day, you would see people going and standing near the windows, closing their eyes and listening to the pigeons.

'So you can actually design your practice in any way you want. Let's take work meetings as an example. We all know meetings can be difficult, challenging, boring. They can be so many things, but they can also be really interesting, right? People often complain they are always in meetings and how meetings are useless. But that is because of the way we construct them. Meetings can be very useful if you take mindfulness into the equation. Take a typical meeting. Somebody is presenting, a few try to listen, others are on their laptops. A few others are on their mobile phones. Even after the meeting has started, nobody is fully present. And then we say, meetings are useless or meetings are inefficient. There's a way to change this.'

Sid chuckled, shaking his head. 'Honestly, Krish, if I got a rupee for every meeting where I saw someone nodding like they're listening but actually scrolling through Instagram under the table, I'd be richer than my CEO by now.'

Krish laughed along. 'Well, if meetings were a sport, multitasking would definitely win gold.'

Multitasking is nothing but doing multiple tasks, equally badly, and at the same time!

Sid couldn't help but laugh. Leaning back, he said. 'Krish, you've officially ruined my LinkedIn bio. I was so proud of calling myself a multitasking expert. Now it sounds like I've been expertly doing things badly all along.'

Krish grinned. 'Well, let's give that title a little makeover, shall we? Here's how you can really excel and turn these meetings into something worth the time.

'To start with, there is a really nice way of arriving at a meeting. Just take a minute to acknowledge that you are fully present. Nobody wants a bad or inefficient meeting but it's just that we don't change our behaviour. Whatever it is that was on your mind before, or whatever it is that you were doing earlier, should be put aside.

'You can also be very clear about defining the agenda for the meeting. Focus on what is happening, finish that and then move on. Trying to send an email and listen to somebody making a presentation at the same time? You are going to do a bad job of both.

'When there is an atmosphere of collective mindfulness, there are great ideas that can come about. People can be positive, creative and build on each other's ideas. We can keep negativity, judgment, criticism and personal agendas out of the meeting. A mindful conversation can begin with making sure that you have understood the other person. I do it a lot of the time. When I hear somebody speak, I say, "Okay, so, what I am hearing from you is . . ." and I kind of rephrase what they said to me. I don't do it every time, but I try it if the topic of the conversation is even slightly complex.

'I allow the other person to make sure that I have understood them. They may add a little more information to my statement. That's how a mindful conversation happens. And at the end of the meeting, just closing with a few moments of thanks and appreciation is a great way to run a successful meeting.'

Sid had a thoughtful smile on his face. 'So, running a mindful meeting isn't just about sticking to an agenda, it's about creating a space where everyone feels heard and ideas can flow freely. It's like building a team rhythm where understanding and positivity set the tone. And ending with gratitude—that's the cherry on top. I really like that, Krish.'

Just then, Sid's stomach growled and he laughed, patting it. 'Well, Krish, all this talk of mindfulness is making me mindful of something very immediate—my hunger! I think my stomach just called for a meeting of its own.'

Krish laughed, 'Ah, Sid, perfect timing! Why don't we use that hunger to dive into another fascinating practice—mindful eating? Let's talk about what it means to truly savour your food.

'To eat mindfully, you can follow a small framework. The first thing to ask yourself is, "Am I hungry or thirsty, or am I eating for the heck of it?" Because many times, that's what we end up doing. You ask someone at lunch time what they had for breakfast. Many people won't know. They have to think, because usually at breakfast, they are already on email or social media. Hardly anyone is just savouring the taste of their food. This framework requires that you notice your feelings and ask yourself: "Why am I eating like this? What is this habit and where is this coming from?"

'My experience with mindful eating has been transformational. I will tell you how it changed my life. When I modified the way I eat, I became healthier. It is not like I suddenly started exercising more. I come from a family of people with hypertension, diabetes and cholesterol. Both my parents had all these lifestyle challenges and so do my siblings. As a child, I was not the healthiest. I used to fall ill quite frequently and get colds and coughs. It persisted well into my twenties. When I started eating like this though, not only did I become fitter, my immunity levels also really improved. I stopped falling ill or catching even a common flu. I say this with a great deal of humility and with a lot of gratitude. I hope that it stays that way.

'I work out every day for about two hours, I have very good energy levels and a lot of this is because of mindful eating. So, what is mindful eating? I am just going to cover this in four simple steps.'

Sid raised an eyebrow, intrigued. 'Wait a minute, Krish. Are you saying that just by changing how you eat—not even *what* you eat—you were able to improve your health, manage your weight and feel better overall? That's kind of incredible! But how does it work? Is it about eating slowly, eating less or just paying more attention?'

Krish smiled knowingly. 'Ah, Sid, it's both simpler and deeper than that. Mindful eating is about much more than just slowing down. It's about understanding the connection between what you eat, how you eat and who you are. Let me explain with the first element—your state.'

Sid leaned forward, his curiosity clearly piqued. 'Okay, you've got my attention. What's this "state" all about?'

'Let me break it down for you,' Krish chuckled.

'The first element of mindful eating is your state. When we are born, we are all roughly the same size and weight. Then, over the next two decades, some of us become six feet or more, some of us five feet something, some are fifty kilos, some are seventy kilos, some are a hundred kilos. Of course there is a genetic disposition to this, but what else is there? The body is nothing but the transformation of the food we consume.

'The body consists of multiple states. What you refer to as "you" is the physical state, mental state, emotional state and the energy state. These are the four states that constitute "you". So now, the food you eat is transforming into "you". So if any of these states are poor or not good, then no matter how organic or high quality the food is, it will also become the same state. It's like taking clean water and pouring it into muddy water. The entire mix will still be muddy!

'So, the first element: what state are you in when you eat? Are you happy, calm, peaceful, aware? Or is there anger or any other negative emotion? Remember, whatever be your existing state, the food will become that state. This is the most important thing to understand.

'The second element is something many of us have been taught as kids—gratitude. We have been taught to have a moment of gratitude and say a prayer. This is a very powerful tool because it immediately alters your state. So just stop for a moment to say thanks because merely doing that with complete focus shifts your thoughts, emotions and energy into a positive state.

'The third element is eating with awareness. I will guide you through it in a moment. It is about looking at your food, not looking at your phone or some screen and mindlessly shoving food into your mouth. Instead, you examine the colour, the texture and the fragrance of food.

'The fourth element is very scientific. It is about chewing. We chew to mix the food with saliva and make it easy to digest. The saliva starts to break the food down into sugars so that the blood absorbs the sugar and you get energy. Digestion is the activity on which we expend the most amount of energy in a day. 70 per cent of our energy goes into digestion. 15–20 per cent goes into running the brain. You use 10–15 per cent for every other activity. With mindful eating, digestion can come down from 70 per cent to less than 50 per cent of energy expended. That means straight away 20 per cent more energy is available to you. Chewing is the most important thing. The scientific explanation here is that it takes twenty minutes for the signal to go from the stomach to the brain saying, "enough". In twenty minutes, many of us can finish not just one meal, but two meals! So, by the time the brain recognizes that it's had enough, you have already overeaten. By chewing and eating slowly, we create an opportunity for the signal to reach the brain. You will notice that you immediately and automatically eat less. As a result, you will have more energy and greater immunity.'

**When you listen to the body, you eat out of need.
Otherwise, you eat out of greed.**

Sid leaned back slightly, his brows furrowing a bit sceptically. 'Wait, Krish, are you saying that how we eat—our state, our gratitude, even how much we chew—can alter how our body processes food and energy? That's wild! I mean, I know digestion is important, but I never thought about it in this much detail.'

Krish grinned. 'Exactly, Sid. It's not just about what you eat but how you eat. The body is a miraculous machine and mindful eating is like giving it the respect it deserves. Curious to experience this for yourself?'

Sid nodded enthusiastically, leaning forward again. 'Of course! I need to see how this works.'

Krish took out a small raisin from his pocket and handed it to Sid. 'Alright, my friend, let's try a little exercise. This is going to be fun!

'So, now just try this. Pick up this raisin and just follow my instructions. First look deeply at it, taking your complete awareness to it. Notice its shape, notice its colour, notice the texture.'

Sid turned the raisin slowly between his fingers, noticing its wrinkled surface and deep, earthy brown hue. The tiny crevices caught the light, giving it an almost jewel-like quality, and he couldn't help but smile at how much detail he had overlooked before.

'Now just touch it with your fingers. How does it feel, is it rough or smooth?' Krish paused.

Sid gently rolled the raisin between his fingers, noticing the slight stickiness and the tiny grooves on its surface. It felt both soft and firm at the same time, sparking a sense of curiosity he hadn't expected from something so small.

'Where did this come from? What was it like originally? This raisin was a smooth, plump, grape and now it is rough, much smaller. What all went into making this? The sun, rain, earth. Reflecting on this, gently and softly close your eyes. Take that little raisin up to your nose and smell it. What is it that you notice? Have you ever smelled a raisin before?' Krish paused.

Sid turned the raisin over gently in his fingers, Krish's questions echoing in his mind. He marvelled at the idea of the sun, rain and earth all contributing to something so small.

Sid closed his eyes, bringing the raisin close to his nose. A subtle, sweet aroma filled his senses, faintly familiar yet intriguing. He realized he'd never truly noticed the smell of a raisin before—it was an extraordinary discovery in something so ordinary.

'Now keeping your eyes closed, just touch it to your lips. What is the texture like? Don't eat it yet. Allow your body and mind to relax. Gently open your mouth and place it on your tongue. Close your mouth but do not bite. Put your hand down. Notice what is happening in your body and mind. Is there suddenly more saliva? Is your stomach growling? Is the mind saying, "Eat, chew it fast, what are you doing?" Simply observe the chatter, don't listen to it.'

As Sid touched the raisin to his lips, he noticed its slightly rough texture, a contrast to its earlier smooth scent. He placed it gently on his tongue, resisting the urge to chew. Almost instantly, he felt a surge of saliva building in his mouth and a faint growl from his stomach, reminding him of his hunger. His mind buzzed with chatter—"Just eat it already!"—but he focused on observing these sensations without giving in, letting Krish's words guide him.

'Now gently squeeze the raisin with your teeth. What is the predominant flavour? Can you taste the sweetness? Is there also a sourness? Don't swallow yet. By now you probably have a bit of saliva in your mouth. So take a few more bites, keeping the juice and saliva in your mouth, chew a few more times, allow it to become paste in your mouth. Don't swallow yet. What's happening in the stomach right now? Is there a lot of growling?

'Is your stomach saying, "Come on, send it to me!"? Don't listen. Keep your awareness in the mouth and slowly, when you are ready, just swallow half of what is in your mouth. Notice it going down your throat. Down, down, down the food pipe till it reaches the stomach. What happens now? Is there a big celebration in the stomach?'

As Sid gently bit into the raisin, its sweetness burst onto his tongue, followed by a faint hint of sourness. He noticed the juices mixing with the saliva in his mouth, creating a surprisingly rich flavour he had never experienced before. His stomach growled impatiently, as if urging him to hurry, but he resisted, staying with the sensations in his mouth.

When he finally swallowed half, he followed its journey, imagining the food pipe carrying it down into his stomach. He couldn't help but chuckle softly as he pictured his stomach celebrating its arrival like a tiny festival.

'Now, bring your awareness back to your mouth. Finish chewing what you have there. Slowly and gently, whenever you are ready, swallow it and again feel it go down all the way. Bring your awareness back to the mouth, using your tongue to clean up what was left and finally swallow the remaining bits. That raisin is well on its way to become a part of your body. So, just thank it for becoming part of you and taking good care of you. Whenever you are ready, softly open your eyes.'

Sid focused on the last remnants of the raisin, savouring every bit as he finished chewing. It was a while before he opened his eyes. He looked at Krish, shaking his head in disbelief.

'Wow! Krish, that was wild! Simply wild! I mean, I've eaten raisins my whole life, but that felt like . . . I don't know, a spiritual experience? Who knew a raisin had so much to say? I don't think I even need lunch anymore. That one raisin feels like it's still sitting there, keeping me completely satisfied. It's bizarre.'

You are what you eat.

Krish laughed heartily, tapping his fingers lightly on his knee. 'And to think it's just one raisin, Sid. Imagine if we brought that level of awareness to an entire meal. But I see that slight look of hesitation on your face—you're wondering how to do this without becoming the "weird guy" at the lunch table, right?'

Sid grinned sheepishly. 'Caught me. I'm imagining my colleagues staring at me, wondering if I've joined some secret cult. How do I even make this work in real life?'

Krish leaned forward, a playful glint in his eye. 'Oh, it's possible. Let's tackle that next. Maybe you can eat one meal a day like this. If that is also not possible, I would ask, "Can you eat at least one or two mouthfuls every day like this, once in a while or every meal?" Before eating, just express gratitude and check in with your body. Make sure the state is good. Nobody is going to object to those things. And then eat with awareness for five minutes before going into the rest of the meal. Or perhaps you can do this once or twice a week.'

'Ah! This is why you eat all your meals in silence. I see you praying, maybe silently thanking the person who has made it, deeply looking into the food, chewing slowly,' Sid said. On more than one occasion, Sid had admired Krish for his obvious fitness and good health. There was an energy to this man that Sid had never seen before. It all suddenly made sense to him now.

'Remember, whether it is brushing your teeth, having a shower, listening to people or eating, they are all wonderful and powerful ways of bringing mindfulness into your life. Mindfulness is pure energy. It's like constantly charging yourself through these activities. So you are like a fully charged device at all times.'

Sid leaned back, his gaze drifting towards the trees swaying gently in the afternoon breeze. Krish's words lingered in his mind, weaving connections between the seemingly mundane acts of daily life and the profound energy of mindfulness.

'So, it's all connected,' Sid murmured, half to himself. 'All these little moments . . . they're not just random chores, are they? They're opportunities.'

Krish smiled knowingly, sensing Sid's reflection. 'Exactly. The power of integrated practice is that it makes even the ordinary extraordinary. Every moment becomes magical.'

Sid's brow furrowed slightly, curiosity sparking. 'But there's so much I still don't understand, Krish. How do I know if I'm doing it right? Can't I mess this up?'

Krish chuckled softly, gesturing for Sid to continue. 'Good. That curiosity is the perfect place to start. Let's open this up—ask me anything that arises without hesitation.'

Sid, now fully engaged and brimming with curiosity, leaned forward with a glint in his eyes. 'Alright, Krish, speaking of eating and drinking, here's a spicy one for you—do our positive or negative thoughts actually transfer into the food we cook?'

Krish raised an eyebrow, clearly enjoying the spark in Sid's demeanour. 'Ah, now that's a question worth chewing on,' he said with a grin. 'Since we're also playing a game of puns, let's stir this pot of ideas and see what flavours emerge.

'I would say, most definitely, YES. Positive and negative thoughts get transferred at multiple stages. Even when you're preparing the ingredients, not just when you're cooking. In fact, it can happen even at the time of harvesting. You can keep going back in the supply chain and you will find that it holds true at every stage. Therefore, it's important to ensure that the person who's cooking is in a positive state of mind with positive emotions. Traditionally, people would have a bath and then start cooking. There would be some music playing in the background and all these were important aspects of ensuring that the food came out well. It's not something that is quite visible but there's enough evidence to suggest that each of these is a very important step.'

Sid tilted his head, 'Doesn't integrating mindfulness slow everything down?'

Krish chuckled, 'Let me explain it in another way.'

'When you started learning to walk, how did you learn? It was by walking slowly. As you got better at it, you started walking faster and faster. And there came a day when you could run. It's the same thing for a language or instrument you learn. When you learn, you learn it slowly. Once you get better at it, you can do it at any speed. The same thing goes for mindfulness. When you start, slowing down is a good way of bringing awareness into the activity. But once you've been practising for a long time, speed is not a factor necessarily. When Usain Bolt is running, what do you think is happening? He's in complete mindfulness. He's in a total state of awareness, right? The stadium doesn't exist. The thousands of people watching him don't exist. His competitors barely exist. There's only him and the ground. And he's running at a speed that most of us can't. So, speed is a factor that can be a little inhibiting in the beginning, but once you get used to it, it is not a problem. In fact, there is a very beautiful Zen saying:

Even when you rush, rush slowly.

'What does that mean? Of course, sometimes you have to rush. If you have to catch a train or a plane and you know you're late, you can't say, "Oh I am in mindfulness now and I'll go very slowly." You'll miss your flight. So, you must rush. But you rush with awareness. That means you don't run into somebody. You don't step on somebody's feet. You don't fall. That's what rushing with awareness means. Start slow. As you become better and better, you can automatically choose to increase the speed.'

Sid shifted his weight slightly, fixing his elbows on his knees as he stared thoughtfully at the ground. 'Rush slowly,' he murmured, letting the phrase roll around in his mind. He pictured Usain Bolt in full sprint, his focus so sharp that the world seemed to melt away—a paradoxical blend of speed and stillness.

'You know, Krish,' Sid began, a contemplative smile playing on his lips, 'it's like you're saying mindfulness isn't about moving at a snail's pace; it's about being fully present, no matter the speed. Whether I'm sprinting to catch a train or brushing my teeth, I can still bring that awareness to what I'm doing.'

He paused, raising his hand to his head, and slowly ran his fingers through his hair, noticing the soft texture and the slight coolness of his fingertips against his scalp. 'It's funny—just paying attention to small things like this feels grounding,' he remarked with a chuckle. 'It's interesting how mindfulness feels like such a slow and deliberate practice at first, but it's really preparing you for life's quick moments, isn't it? It's like building the foundation for awareness that doesn't waver, no matter how fast or chaotic things get.'

Krish nodded, his smile widening. 'Exactly, Sid. It's not about changing the pace of life—it's about changing the quality of how you experience it.'

Krish stretched his arms above his head and glanced at Sid. 'Why don't we take a short walk as we dive into the next question?' he suggested with a grin. Sid nodded, standing up and stretching his shoulders.

As they stood up, the crisp afternoon breeze greeted them. They paused silently for a moment, taking in the vibrant rustling of the leaves and the distant hum of birdsong.

Sid pointed towards a butterfly flitting gracefully among the flowers. 'Look at that,' he said softly. 'So much movement, yet it feels so calm.'

Krish smiled, his gaze following the butterfly. 'That's nature's way, Sid. Perfect focus amidst all the chaos. A lesson in itself.'

Sid chuckled. 'Speaking of focus, here's something I've been curious about. How do we deal with distractions or noise while meditating? Any secret tricks there?' he asked, turning back to Krish with a raised eyebrow.

Krish turned, his eyes gleaming with readiness. 'Great question,' he replied, leading Sid on a walk.

'When you are a beginner, perhaps a certain level of silence may be required. And that is just like learning anything else. You need a specific setting for it. So in an urban environment, you can always use earphones. There are so many ways of achieving less noise or noiselessness. But that is only in the beginning. As you become better at it, do you really need everything else to stop around you? In an orchestra, there are so many musicians playing so beautifully. They are hearing their music and they are also fully aware of everything else that's going on around them. So, there are different levels of meditation. In the beginning, it might help in some forms of meditation to have silence. In fact, in the yogic system of meditation, concentration is the basic requirement. It's called *dharana* which means concentration on one object. So, in those kinds of settings, maybe silence is helpful.

'But as your practice deepens, there comes *dhyana*. That means you are conscious of all the noises around you and yet you are aware of yourself. So, you can hear the traffic outside on the road, you can hear other people speaking, you're conscious of everything and yet you are not carried away by any single thing. That is what dhyana means. Remember,

Real meditation is not how you sit with your eyes closed.
Real meditation is how you live your life.

'That is the essence, the true objective or goal of all meditation. Remember the outcome and just go with the flow. That said, in the beginning, when you are just starting out, some amount of silence is helpful. However, do not get too attached to the process and end up forgetting everything else.'

Sid leaned forward, 'Any tips on mindful listening when we can't see the other person? Like during virtual calls or phone conversations?'

Krish nodded thoughtfully, a small smile forming. 'Ah, an interesting one. Let's explore that, shall we?' He took a deep breath, ready to share his insights.

'What happens when you listen to your favourite music? You automatically close your eyes, isn't it? Why does that happen? It is because there is so much distraction through the eyes that when you close them, your attention goes to the sensation of sound. So, sometimes actually being able to listen without seeing can be an advantage. Of course, that said, there are other advantages when you are able to see, including being able to observe body language and facial expressions. When you're listening, give it your complete attention and do not get too distracted by the sense of sight.'

'Like that time I was talking to the person sitting next to me on a flight,' Sid laughed sheepishly. 'I barely listened to her because I was too distracted by the view from the window!'

'Listening with complete attention to a voice can give much deeper insights. For example, customer care professionals are trained to smile when they speak on the phone because even though you can't see them, you feel the smile communicated through their voice.'

Sid leaned forward with a smile. 'Alright, Krish, here's my final question for the afternoon—how can mindfulness help with sleeping soundly? After all this talk of energy and focus, it seems like the perfect note to end on.'

Krish laughed warmly, clearly enjoying Sid's enthusiasm. 'Ah, the art of restful sleep. A fitting conclusion indeed,' he said, settling back with a thoughtful expression.

'If you spend your entire day in mindfulness, then there'll be absolutely no problem when it's time to sleep. A really good way to do it is to just lie down and take your awareness to your body. Take a few deep breaths and then do a simple body scan starting with your feet. Just notice the different body parts and use your awareness to relax any tightness and tension. Many times, by the time you come up to your head, you will already be asleep.'

'That sounds simple enough. Although I'm sure it's not that easy to keep the mind from wandering. I'm definitely going to try it tonight!' Sid enthused.

* * *

Later, as the day wound down, the golden hues of the setting sun bathed the veranda in a warm glow. Sid leaned back in his chair, sipping the last of his green tea, his mind abuzz with thoughts.

Krish stretched lazily and stood up, glancing at Sid with a knowing smile. 'Sid,' he said, his voice calm yet invigorating, 'you've taken in quite a lot today. Why don't you take some time to reflect and let it all settle? A good night's sleep will seal the lessons for you.'

Sid nodded, the weight of the day's insights feeling less like a burden and more like a treasure to unpack. 'I think I'll do just that, Krish. Thanks for everything today.'

Saying that, Sid headed to his motorcycle. He was going to put Krish's integrated mindfulness practice techniques to a test. Sid reached into the saddle bag and pulled out two pieces of cleaning cloth. He had always kept two. One for dusting the bike and the other for wet wiping it. He then got two small buckets of water.

Sid picked up the dusting cloth and began. He worked carefully and stepped back to check his progress. One area under the speedometer was still dusty and Sid attended to it.

Once he was satisfied, he picked up the wet cloth and started wiping the headlight and then the handlebars of the bike. He did this with utmost concentration. Each little speck of dirt was catching his attention and he made sure that he was soaking it and removing it. In this way, Sid worked on wiping the motorcycle clean, part by little part.

In the past, he would just throw a lot of water at the wheels and cursorily wipe them down. This time, it was different. Sid sat down next to the wheels and wiped the rims clean. He then wiped the spokes. One by one.

The Screaming Eagle pipes were dirty. As he started to clean them, he paid attention to every little bit of mud stuck to them. Once done, he reviewed them again. Unhappy with a dull patch, Sid bent down and frosted the silencer with his breath before polishing it further with the long sleeve of his shirt.

Finally, Sid stepped back and walked all around the motorcycle to inspect it.

Paying attention to anything like this was a new experience and that he would do it with the mundane job of cleaning was something he had never imagined in his wildest dreams.

He noticed a sense of relaxation in his body although he had done physical work. There was also a feeling of accomplishment.

Wow! Imagine if I could do every job with this degree of attention and be able to produce this quality of output, Sid thought to himself. He did not know at that moment that this discovery was going to alter the very course of his life.

Sid got to his room and looked out of the window. The large tree in the distance looked majestic in the light of dusk.

He picked up his journal. The cool evening breeze blew in to greet him like it was eager to add crispness to his writing. Sid closed his eyes and felt the breeze on his face. The bamboo leaves rustled.

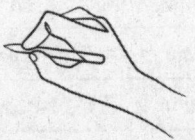

Today felt like peeling back the layers of an onion—simple on the outside but revealing so much depth within.

Mindfulness is a form of energy.

Everyday moments—brushing my teeth, showering, walking—can be transformed into opportunities to create this energy. It's like discovering hidden power sources scattered throughout my day!

I often miss what's being said as well as what's not being said because I'm not listening deeply.

Mindful eating was a game-changer. Who knew a raisin could teach me so much?

Multitasking is 'doing multiple things equally badly, and at the same time!'.

Mindfulness isn't slowing me down; it's about sharpening my focus and creating clarity.

Integrating mindfulness into my life isn't about adding tasks to my day. It's about transforming the tasks I already do. It's about bringing energy, intention and presence to every moment.

I feel lighter, energized and strangely excited for tomorrow. It's not often that life's simplicity feels this profound.

Mindfulness is not something you do. It is a state you are in, no matter what you do.

Eating isn't just about food; it's about my relationship with what nourishes me. The four pillars—state, gratitude, awareness and chewing—make so much sense now.

My little practices:

1. Brush my teeth mindfully and extend this practice to my morning shower.
2. Practise mindful listening during my next call or conversation.
3. Integrate mindful eating—start with gratitude and chew slowly.
4. Experiment with mindful walking, even if it's just to pick up a coffee.

> 5. Try the body scan before sleeping and reflect on how it feels.
>
> **Reflection question:** Where else in my daily routine can I start to practise mindfulness?

Sid set his journal down, took a deep breath and looked out the window at the stars dotting the night sky. They winked back at him knowing he was uncovering powerful secrets.

That night, Sid felt ready to embrace sleep—not as an escape, but as a continuation of the mindfulness he was learning to live with.

Day 6: Values, Motivation and Manifesting a Life of Meaning

Sid sat across Krish and sipped his tea, trying to enjoy its taste as some of the thoughts he had been avoiding in the last few months whirled around in his head. He finally turned to Krish and said, 'You know, when I started my career, I was happy and highly motivated. But then, I don't know what happened. As time passed, it changed. These days I don't even feel like going to work. I've been hearing similar feelings from colleagues who have been working for fifteen–twenty years. Most of them just seem to be mindlessly moving along.

'I often ask them, "Why didn't you fix this?" And the answer I get is, "I don't know how and where to begin." Personally, I tried positive thinking, I tried to motivate myself, but it didn't last. Is this how life is?'

Day 6: Values, Motivation and Manifesting a Life of Meaning

Krish smiled. It was a while before he responded, 'No, life does not have to be this way. Life is beautiful and you can live each day with great joy. The motivation to live like this doesn't come from attending a motivational programme or listening to a fifteen-minute YouTube video. That might make you feel good for maybe a day or two. Then life goes back to how it's always been. You have to use your awareness and understand motivation at a deeper level. When that happens, motivation becomes sustainable.

'Actually when we say motivation, one of the first things people think of is money. I don't have a problem with that, but let me ask you this. After you acquire all the comfort money can buy you, what will you do?' Krish paused, looking intently at Sid. However, it didn't seem like he was expecting an answer. 'You will get bored,' he said and Sid nodded in understanding.

'This is a fact that's been established by some of the richest people on the planet. After a certain amount, money doesn't matter all that much. Money can give you a pleasant life, though. As Bill Gates once said, "I can understand wanting to have millions of dollars, there's a certain freedom, meaningful freedom, that comes with that. But once you get beyond that, I have to tell you, it's the same hamburger."

'I'll explain this with an example. Say, you want to have a hot shower. As soon as you step into the shower, you find it relaxing. But after a while, you want to come out. Life is like this. You enjoy the pleasures in it, but after a while, you want something else.

'There is something beyond a life of luxury that is more sustainable. It's a life of engagement. A kind of life where you use your skills, play to your strengths, and expand your capabilities in a very good way. You engage with tasks, engage with your life, engage with your career, your parenting, or your role as a son, daughter, spouse or partner. An engaging life can take you beyond material stuff. It is the next level of life.

'But I believe that even an engaging life can be made better. I think there is something beyond even that—a meaningful life. I believe it happens when you start working towards a purpose. The purpose being something larger than yourself.

'Think about it for yourself. The people you know who live very meaningful lives, what are they doing? Chances are, yes, there is a certain amount of money. They live an engaged life, but they are very likely involved with something a little bigger than themselves. A bigger cause. They could be creating something new, building an organization, serving a cause, helping to protect the environment. Such people are more likely to be truly happy with what they are doing, and that's what makes for a meaningful life.'

'Does wanting to be more successful not count? Could wanting career growth and money, a bigger house and a fancier car, not give me meaning?' Sid asked tentatively, knowing that the answer was likely to be 'no'.

Krish laughed as his eyes twinkled mischievously. 'Why don't we discover the answer to that question together?' he asked Sid.

'You say success. What does "success" mean? When you were one year old, it meant learning how to walk. Later, it meant not wetting your pants. At eighteen, it meant getting a driver's license and having a girlfriend. A few years later, it meant completing your education. And then, it became about money and career growth, a bigger house and a fancier car, didn't it? But did that satisfy you?'

'No, not really,' acknowledged Sid.

'Right. I suspect riding your motorcycle gives you a greater sense of freedom! You see, at every point, your definition of success changes. In fact, there will come a time when success will again mean not wetting your pants and being able to walk! So "success" is subjective. It means different things at different points in life and can mean different things to different people. It is important. I don't deny that. But I believe you can apply the concepts of mindfulness we have discussed to start shaping your life to become more meaningful in addition to being successful.

'Have you heard about the candle problem? It was created by a psychologist called Karl Duncker. He took people into a room and gave them a candle, a box full of board pins, and a match box. They had to fix the candle to the wall in such a way that the wax would not drip on the ground.

'Most people took the pins and tried to stick the candle to the wall with the pin. After some time, the candle fell. Others figured out that if you removed all the pins from the box, you could actually pin the box to the wall. They then lit the candle and kept it in the box for the candle wax to collect. Different people figured this out in different ways.

'Roughly twenty years later, another man named Sam Glucksberg brought a new layer of complexity into this experiment. He asked two groups of people to do the experiment. To the first group, he said, "We are going to observe you and time you to see how soon you figure it out." To the other group, he gave a target and a reward. He said, "If you do it in a certain number of minutes, you are going to get so many dollars." Surprisingly, the second group took three and half minutes longer than the first group!

'What does this tell you? Money is not always a right motivator or even a great motivator. Money works, but in certain kinds of situations. Like money, there are several external or extrinsic motivators. In the case of the candle problem, the group that was told that they were simply going to be measured to set a standard aligned with something internal to them—maybe a sense of self-worth. These are intrinsic or internal motivators. For example, some of my important motivators are freedom, justice, fair play, a sense of honesty, fairness and creativity.

'In my opinion, external motivators, including money, are good for left brain functions. In the industrial revolution money was a good incentive for repetitive jobs that required efficiency. But today, in the 21st century we are constantly problem-solving. These are mostly right brain functions, which require intrinsic motivators. I will tell you a story.

'I know someone who graduated from one of the world's best business schools and got an amazing job. He had a beautiful apartment and a swanky company car. He was comfortable in every respect. It was quite a pleasant life, even a slightly engaging life. But you know what happened? Over time, he became deeply unhappy. Though he didn't know it immediately, it was because he wasn't able to satisfy any of his intrinsic motivators. He was successful on the outside. Empty inside.

'As he reflected on this at length, he started to realize a few things. He valued autonomy: the independence or freedom to explore, to be, to discover. That holds true for all of us. Nobody likes to be suffocated and put in a cage. He craved mastery: he looked at his life and wondered where he excelled. He realized it was his ability to see simplicity in complexity. To see complex patterns and then be able to break them down into smaller and more understandable parts.

'He then realized he wanted a sense of purpose too. So, it became a question of how to combine autonomy and mastery with a sense of purpose. From a young age, helping other people was really important to him. He loved supporting others and it gave him enormous satisfaction. He understood that this was his purpose and he had to align it with his desires.

'His current job gave him none of these to the extent he needed. That day, he decided he had to change something. You know what they say, if you find something you love doing, you never have to work another day in your life? That is exactly what happened to him. Over the years that followed, this philosophy became the lighthouse that guided him. He started doing work that he found deeply meaningful and engaging. He stopped "working".'

Sid couldn't help but wonder if this was Krish's own story but something kept him from asking.

'Sometimes we get so caught up in doing something that we lose track of time. It could be a sport you are playing, an instrument, music you are listening to or even a presentation you are working on. Some people write code like that. When you lose track of time, when there is a sense of effortlessness, of forgetting the self, there is a certain richness to the experience that is almost indescribable. What if you could be in that state all the time? Is it possible? Yes!'

Krish's words stirred something in Sid. He shifted slightly, his gaze falling on the flickering lantern at the edge of the veranda. A memory surfaced—a moment from his college days when he was painting a mural for a campus event.

It had started as a simple task, but as Sid lost himself in the strokes of the brush, time seemed to dissolve. He remembered the colours blending effortlessly, his focus so intense that he barely noticed his friends coming and going around him or even his own hunger. By the time he stepped back to look at his work, the sun had set and his muscles ached from standing so long but he felt nothing but satisfaction.

Sid smiled faintly, running a hand through his hair. 'You know, Krish, I remember this one time in college, painting a mural. Hours went by, and I didn't even notice. It was just . . . pure joy. I haven't felt that in years.'

Krish's eyes lit up with recognition. 'Ah, the state of flow. That's when who you are and what you're doing align so seamlessly that time itself feels irrelevant. And yet, so many lose touch with that feeling. Do you know why, Sid?'

Sid leaned in, curious, as Krish continued. 'It's because we lose alignment—between who we are and what motivates us. Let's dive into this together.

'There are a few steps to find this state. To start with, we need to find alignment between who we are and what our motivators are. A lot of people become unhappy with what they are doing and the way their lives are because they have not made this alignment. They are like square pegs forever trying to fit into round holes.

'Somebody told them to become an engineer or a doctor or an accountant and that's what they did. They just followed that path without understanding if that connected to who they really were. You must find alignment between your intrinsic motivators and who you are, so that motivation is constant and sustainable. If you truly enjoy what you are doing, there is no need to generate motivation as it will come organically.

'The next thing—it is important to find the right balance between your skills and the challenges you find in life. Imagine your skills are low but your challenges are very high, what will happen? You are going to have stress and anxiety, because your skills are not equipped to deal with those challenges. On the other hand, if your skills are very high, but there are no challenges, you will be terribly bored. So balancing these with awareness is key.

'Now the trick is to remain in the middle. The secret is to keep increasing the challenges and improving your skills on a constant basis. Imagine you are throwing darts at a board. Over time, you get really good at it. You'll hit bullseye every time. What would you do then? You'd perhaps move further away. Or throw with the other hand. It's the same thing with life! You have to keep challenging yourself. That is when you truly come alive!

'To find a high degree of alignment you also need to be clear about your values. How do you do this? Pick up that notepad and pen,' Krish pointed to a nearby table.

'Think of three people you admire,' he continued once Sid had the pad ready. 'They could be real or fictional. People you know or don't. Against each of their names, list three to five traits of theirs that you admire. For example, I really like Spiderman, particularly for his cool sense of humour. Even when he is stuck in a difficult situation, he sees humour in it.

'Once you do this, you'll have ten to fifteen traits. From these, pick five that you have. These could be traits that you already have or wish to have more of.'

There was silence as Sid wrote.

'There you are. These are your values. Typically we tend to admire the values in people that we either have or we wish we had. By identifying your values, you are one step closer to building intrinsic and sustainable motivation.' Krish continued when Sid indicated that he was done. 'Now you can start to see whether your life currently, or the life you wish to build, is really in sync with your values. But before that, let me tell you a story I've heard. I have not personally verified it but it is a good story!

'This is about someone in the USA. The lady had a good job, stable income. Life was good. One day, she read about an exercise to gauge satisfaction in life. All she had to do was write her own obituary. She decided to give it a try. As she wrote, she started to get really sad. She wasn't able to write it beyond a point because she realized she found her life boring. She then began to think how her life could be if she were to do everything she really wanted to do. This exercise was so exciting and so interesting that she couldn't stop writing!

'Eventually she got so motivated that she bought a boat and became the first person to row solo across the Atlantic. Forty-five days into the journey, her stove broke down and one of her oars broke. But she went on to complete it. Later, she became the first person to row solo across the Pacific as well. Roz Savage became an inspiration to many.'

'Wow!' exclaimed Sid. 'This is an exercise I think I should really try!'

'When we start to tap into what our values really are, something amazing starts to happen. We start to live life according to those values, creating experiences of value to us. And that is what true motivation is all about—living a meaningful life,' Krish continued.

'And yes. I'd like you to discover your ideal future too, Sid. I want you to think what your life will be like in two to three years if everything you wish for happens. I want you to write this down. Only then can you know who you are and what you want to do.

'Imagine everything today that you asked for comes true. It could be with respect to your career, your relationships, money, where you live, etc. You could be a CEO or you could be an author, or you could be an actor. You could be a social worker; you could be anything. Use your values to build your future. How would you feel if you were living this life?'

'Write it down in detail in your journal when you can,' Krish urged Sid

'People can use this exercise to transform their lives. You don't necessarily have to sell all your possessions and travel across the world on your bike. You can create a significant impact even through what you are doing right now.'

Krish went on to tell Sid a story of someone he had met a few years ago. The person worked at a consumer goods company and he was passionate about improving standards of hygiene in poor countries. He envisioned a future in which he would be at the forefront of a movement that would drive this change. One day, he bought a bar of soap and kept it on his desk. He would look at it every day. It was a constant reminder of what he wanted to achieve. Over the next year, he helped his company acquire a soap manufacturer in Africa and eventually became its CEO. By keeping that bar of soap in a place so he could see it every day, he was reminding himself of the future he had envisioned. It propelled him to act and make that future come true.

'You too can do this if you like Sid,' Krish said as Sid's eyes lit up with excitement. He leaned forward, eager to soak in every word. The idea of envisioning his future and actively shaping it resonated deeply. He felt a bolt of energy coursing through him, a kind he hadn't felt in years.

Krish noticed Sid's enthusiasm and smiled knowingly. 'Hold onto that energy, Sid. Let's take a moment to turn this into something tangible.' Krish gestured towards a shaded spot under a large tree nearby, where the dappled sunlight danced on the ground. The air was calm, punctuated by the occasional chirping of birds.

'Come,' Krish said, picking up a small mat from a nearby bench and laying it under the tree. 'This is the perfect spot for a little introspection.'

Sid followed, settling himself on the mat. The cool shade of the tree contrasted with the warm breeze, creating a soothing balance. He adjusted his posture, grounding himself in the moment.

Believe now that you will become that future self.
Desire deeply now that future self.
Accept now that you are already taking the first step towards becoming that future self.

'The first step is to clearly write down what you have just envisioned as a future. Break this vision down into a set of life goals across a few important categories. So, for example, you could have "improved health" as a category, or work, even relationships. Under each of these, you must put down some goals. When you write this down in such a granular manner, you start to form a detailed picture of how you would like different areas of your life to be.

'Once you have written these down, it is important for you to read this repeatedly for a few days. When you repeatedly read it, you are further installing it in your mind. What happens next is fascinating even at a scientific level. There is a part of your brain called the default mode network or DMN which creates rumination and self-referential thinking when you are idle. The repetition of this exercise is telling the DMN that this is something that means a great deal to you. What happens next is nothing short of incredible. Your brain will call upon all kinds of powers to make your dreams come true.

'At many levels unknown to you, it starts to initiate actions that start taking you in the direction of the dream. When you are sleeping, even your subconscious is looking for ways to make these things come true. Remember how you started to notice more Honda cars once you decided to buy one?

'What follows then is that at a daily level you will, both consciously and unconsciously, end up doing a number of things in service of this manifestation. You further strengthen the process by consciously building out a daily routine that includes micro rituals to take you in the direction of your goals. For example, if good health is a part of your vision you will then create a daily routine that involves enough exercise, sleep and a good diet. If maintaining good relationships is one of your goals, you will make time for those relationships and do the things that are important to nurture them. You will automatically, at a subconscious level, end up doing tiny things that will all add up eventually into a great force!

'Slowly but surely, everything starts to move in the direction of your vision. You manifest the future you desire.'

We are very good in our preparation to live but we have difficulty living in the present.
We take fifteen to twenty years to get ourselves a good education and then we forget to live.
We spend years trying to make money so that we can have a good life, and then we forget to live.
The only way to live is by being in the present moment.
Because that is the ONLY moment in which we can be alive.

'Now, here's the next step to turbocharge your genie. You must tell others about your dream. The more people you tell about it, the more powerful it gets. It's a snowball effect. It starts to gather more and more momentum. At a human level, we all love helping other people. Sharing this with your colleagues, your family and your friends is a really powerful way of making that dream come true.'

The crisp air seemed to hold Krish's words up a little longer as Sid gazed at the sky and marvelled at its vastness, much like the idea that Krish had spoken about. He felt both inspired and a bit hesitant as the sheer magnitude of designing his life slowly started emerging.

Finally, breaking the silence, Sid turned to Krish, his brow furrowed in thought. 'This sounds incredibly powerful,' he began, 'but I can't help wondering . . . isn't mindfulness about being in the present? Should I not stop myself from yearning for a future that is years away?'

Krish replied, 'That is a very good question and I understand your confusion. Does mindfulness mean I cannot think about the past? Does being in the present mean I cannot plan for the future? No, it does not mean that. Mindfulness only tells you not to obsess about the past or the future. The energy of mindfulness comes from being in the present moment and then that energy can be used in a dynamic way to gain deep insights from the past and shape the future.

'When you have to think about the past to learn your lessons, think about the past. But spending your entire time ruminating about the past is futile. Finish reflecting with a calm mind and come back to the present moment, to focus on what is happening right now. Similarly, when you need to plan ahead, whether it's for yourself, your department, your company or family, do think about the future. But then come back to being in the present. It is in living each moment with awareness that you are embracing life and helping co-create your future. If you're constantly in the future or in the past, you're completely missing out on life.'

> **'To the mind that is still, the whole universe surrenders.'—Lao Tzu**

'You can even have a talisman that reminds you occasionally of what you're trying to be or achieve. For the CEO I spoke of earlier, it was a bar of soap. For you, it needs to be oriented to your vision.'

'But what if it takes me some time to build that image of my future?' Sid asked.

'Your vision is not set in stone. Your idea of your ideal self can evolve as you work on it. It's work in progress. It's like the clay being moulded on the wheel. As you create, you may get some further ideas on how to improve your vision. That's how you go with the flow. If you get too rigid, it can cause stress.

'The objective is to have a clear idea and be obsessed with it. But also keep working on it and allow life to build on it. Allow other people to also shape it. When you have this vision and you keep revisiting it, you will also start to see small wins and small signs that tell you that you are moving in that direction.'

Achieve a state of flow doing the things you love.
And also go with the flow of life.
This paradox will create a life of richness.

Sid leaned back as his mind absorbed Krish's words. Then he slowly nodded.

'So, mindfulness doesn't mean ignoring the past or avoiding the future,' Sid began, his tone thoughtful. 'It's about being in the present moment, using that clarity to reflect on the past when needed, and to plan skilfully for the future. The key is not to get stuck there—whether it's ruminating about what's already happened or obsessing over what's yet to come.'

'Yes, exactly,' Krish paused, tapping his fingers lightly on his knee. 'It's like living in the now with purpose. You envision your future, build a vision that inspires you, but you don't live in the future. You live here, in the present, and focus on doing your best right now. That's what helps you manifest that future.'

Sid smiled as an analogy clicked in his mind. 'It's like moulding clay, right? You start with an idea, but as you shape it, the process reveals new possibilities. Your vision evolves and you adapt while staying committed to the essence of what you're creating. It's a balance between holding on to the vision and allowing life to shape it.'

He glanced at Krish. 'Being in a state of flow while also going with the flow—it's like two sides of the same coin, isn't it?' Sid said softly with a quiet sense of wonder.

The stars twinkled in the sky like the revelations of the day and were a gentle reminder that darkness was slowly cloaking them. The occasional rustle of leaves punctuated the steadily growing hum of the crickets.

'We are born with a few choices already made for us. Like our family, our DNA, the way we look, etc. Beyond that, as we grow up, other choices get made for us by our parents. But after a certain stage, we become responsible for the choices we make,' Krish broke the silence eventually.

Choices have consequences.
And those consequences in turn beget more choices.
And so we weave the fabric of life.

'Making choices with awareness creates more favourable consequences, in turn setting up the stage for further choices. Nature *and* nurture play a complex dance creating patterns that reach far beyond what our rational mind is capable of seeing. And as your thoughts flow into your words which flow into your actions, you are shaping your destiny. With awareness, you have more choice to write your destiny than you imagine. The universe is actually waiting for you to co-create your life, your future!'

Sid marvelled at the lucidity of this explanation. He had always wondered if life was destined or if there was free will and the interplay between the two. This was by far the most elegant explanation he had found.

Krish stretched eventually and stood, brushing the dust from his pants. 'Sid,' he said with a warm smile, 'you've had a lot to process today. Why don't you take some time to sit with these thoughts? Let them settle. Perhaps you can jot them down and see what emerges.'

Sid nodded, his mind still whirring with fragments of insights and realizations. 'I think I will,' he said quietly. 'Thank you, Krish. Today has been . . . eye-opening.'

Krish simply placed a hand on Sid's shoulder, a gesture of reassurance, before heading back to the cottage. Sid remained for a moment longer, gazing at the soft glow of the lanterns swaying in the gentle breeze.

Sid turned slowly away and started walking back. He took each step deliberately and with complete awareness of his feet pressing into the earth, the weight of the body shifting to the other leg as he moved forward. The rhythm of his steps was accompanied by the gentle rise and fall of his breath.

The air felt cool to his skin as though it was laced with the moisture of the earth and the scent of wild jasmine. The sounds around him felt like a backdrop as each step he took pulled him closer to the present moment. The walk was no more about reaching a destination but about going deeper into a beautiful experience.

When Sid walked into his room, he immediately felt the coolness of the floor welcoming him back. As he sat at the desk by the window, he felt the chair creak gently as it grounded him. He pulled out his journal. The night air wafted in, carrying with it the faint scents of outside. He opened a blank page, took a deep breath and began to write. The world became quieter. The wind was still as it waited to learn the secrets Sid had uncovered that day.

Day 6: Values, Motivation and Manifesting a Life of Meaning

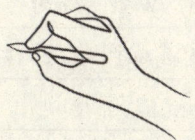

Today, I felt like pieces of a puzzle finally started to fall into place.

Mindfulness doesn't mean ignoring the past or avoiding the future. It's about being in the present and using that clarity to reflect or plan without getting stuck there.

You start with an idea, a vision, but as you shape it, life naturally brings new opportunities and challenges that refine it. Staying committed to the essence of your vision while being open to change—that's the sweet spot.

Who I am and what I do must feel aligned and seamless.

I can build a vision for my future, grounded in my values, and still live fully in the present. One step at a time, with awareness and intention.

Choices have consequences. And those create more choices again. And in understanding this and living each moment with awareness, choosing my thoughts, words and actions, I have the power to design my destiny!

Tomorrow, I'll start shaping that life. For now, I'll just breathe.

My little practice:

Breathing in, I check in with my body. Breathing out, I relax my body.

Breathing in, I check in with my mind. Breathing out, I relax my mind.

Breathing in, I ask myself what's the most important thing for me in this moment. Breathing out, I notice the response that arises.

Reflection questions:

What are a few choices I can make today to start living closer to the life I envision?

What areas of my life have I procrastinated in?

What is holding me back from living my dreams?

In what ways can I see myself living my dreams and loving it?

Sid stood by the window for a moment, gazing at the moonlit landscape. The stillness of the night mirrored the calm he felt within—a quiet yet powerful sense of clarity.

As he climbed into bed, Sid allowed himself a small smile. For the first time in a long while, he felt like the next day held promise, not pressure. Closing his eyes, he let the day's reflections settle, trusting that they would guide him when the morning came.

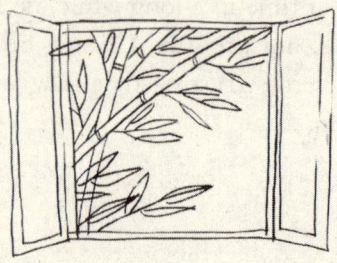

Day 7: Bend, Not Break: A Fluid Quality of Resilience

Sid stretched lazily as the first light of dawn shimmered into his room. The gentle stillness of the night still lingered as the birds started waking up to the day. Sid swung his legs out of bed, determined that he would take a sense of mindfulness to even the smallest of actions.

He picked up his toothbrush with a deliberate action and noticed the coolness of the water as he rinsed the brush. The minty aroma of the toothpaste and the rough texture of the bristles were acute sensations as he experienced them with heightened awareness. Each move of the brush was slow and Sid was in tune with every sensation in his mouth. As he slowly finished, Sid felt a sense of calm with an underlying feeling of peace. It was almost as if the seemingly mundane act of cleaning his teeth had uncovered something precious.

'May my words be as fresh and fragrant too,' he vowed.

Sid stepped out of his room, the morning sunlight warming his face as he took in the serene surroundings of the cottage. The air was still crisp, carrying the faint smell of dew and earth, and the distinct hum of nature created a tranquil backdrop.

As he walked down the gravel path, he noticed Krish standing by his motorbike, running a hand over the handlebars and admiring it thoughtfully.

Krish turned as Sid approached, a smile spreading across his face. 'This is a beauty; I see you've cleaned it,' he said, gesturing to the shiny machine. 'You don't just ride this—you have a relationship with it, don't you?'

'You could say that. It's been with me through a lot—many great rides and a few tough falls.' Sid chuckled, running his fingers over the bike's polished surface.

'Speaking of which,' he added, his tone shifting to one of reflection, 'I've been doing some thinking. Yesterday's conversation really got me reflecting on my journey and what I want for the future. But it also made me wonder—what do I do when obstacles come up? How do I deal with falls, setbacks and failures?'

Krish leaned against the bike, his expression calm but curious. 'Ah, a question worth exploring,' he said. 'Let's talk about that.'

He motioned for Sid to join him on the porch, where they settled into the wooden chairs, the morning light casting dappled patterns around them. Krish began, his voice steady and inviting.

'Yesterday we spoke about finding alignment with your values and discovering intrinsic motivation. As you do this, you start envisioning an ideal future for yourself and even manifesting that future.

'But if there is one thing you can be sure of, it is that there will be challenges. You might have this vision of where you want to get to but you have no idea which path to take. So, how do we cope with this? What do you do when there are challenges, setbacks, even failures as you embark on your journey?

'The one thing you will definitely need is resilience. You must be mentally prepared to deal with difficult times. Usually, resilience is defined as the ability to bounce back, recover or adjust to a challenge, misfortune or change. Everybody intuitively understands the meaning of resilience. We all have resilience already to some extent.

'It is not merely a human capability. Anything that has life has resilience wired into its DNA. Look around you. That blade of grass you stepped on a minute ago is demonstrating resilience. As is that bamboo tree outside your window, bending in the wind. And so is that plant growing in that crack on the wall next to you!'

Sid reached out and gently caressed the tiny plant growing in a crack in the wall, feeling its rough edges and surprisingly sturdy stem. Its quiet strength brought a smile to his face. He looked around him with a fresh perspective as he started to understand what Krish meant.

'What comes to your mind when you think of resilience? We all know of many people who were down and out but managed to bounce back, right? One of my favourite stories of resilience is from the Rocky series. In one of the films, Rocky tells his son, "It ain't about how hard you hit. It's

Day 7: Bend, Not Break: A Fluid Quality of Resilience

about how hard you can get hit and keep moving forward. That's how winning is done!"

'I think there is a lot more to resilience. Grit and determination are certainly important aspects. But just blind grit or mere bull-headed determination are not always good things by themselves.

'Imagine you come across a well in a desert. You see that there is no water in it, but you believe that you can find it. You start digging, going deeper and deeper. You don't find any water, so you put in more effort and you dig some more. Eventually you get exhausted and you still haven't found water. What would you do? Continue digging? Where would you draw the line? When would you say, "Look, I am thinking really positively but I am not finding water here. Perhaps I need to approach this differently. Maybe I should walk over that hill and see if I can find water somewhere else?"

'Resilience is a wonderful thing. But sometimes, we need to bring a greater degree of awareness to it. You need to go beyond being relentlessly positive and find awareness. When you bring awareness in, things starts to change. When you start to bring awareness into determination and grit, they start to evolve. Then you start to build another kind of resilience. One where you don't just bounce back from setbacks and challenges but actually use them to build qualities and skills. When the setback or challenge has passed, these skills can become your superpowers and allow you to not just survive, but thrive! Think of this as Resilience Plus.'

Sid shifted his weight in the chair, his gaze fixed on the horizon. The image of the desert lingered in his mind as he pondered Krish's words. 'So, it's not just about perseverance,' he murmured, half to himself. 'It's also about knowing when to adapt and how to grow from the struggle.' He turned to Krish, 'Do you have an example of this?'

'Let me tell you a story of the American Bald Eagle. I've heard different versions of this story and some even say it is not a true story. I say it doesn't matter; it's a nice story.

'After about twenty-five to thirty years of its life, the eagle's beak starts breaking, talons and nails start wearing out. So, when the eagle is about thirty years of age, it has to make a choice. If it continues the same way, it will probably not live long because it can't hunt anymore. So, they say the eagle actually flies off into the mountains and makes itself a nest on a cliff. It then eats well for a few weeks and prepares itself. Finally, when it is ready, it goes to the nest and bangs its beak against the rock. The beak breaks since it is already weak.

'The beak takes time to grow back. So, the story has it that the eagle starves for about forty-five days till the beak grows back. Then the eagle uses its beak to remove its nails and feathers. These then grow back in another month or so. So, for almost three months, the bird can't hunt. It is quite defenceless. It is almost hibernating.

'But after the beak, nails and feathers have grown back, this eagle can live for many more years. This is a perfect example of resilience because the bird is making a conscious choice to go through extreme difficulty to extend its life span. Whether it's true or not, it makes for a great example of how awareness can shape the choices that we make in difficult situations.

'Now how does this work in the human context? This kind of resilience has a few parts to it. You are already familiar

Day 7: Bend, Not Break: A Fluid Quality of Resilience

with some of them. The first part is inner calm. The second one is emotional resilience, which is about managing your emotions. You have already learnt about those two. Let's understand the third part of adaptive resilience, cognitive resilience.

'Cognitive resilience comes from our internal narrative. It is the story we tell ourselves. You are constantly explaining the events and circumstances of your life to yourself and other people. What goes into this narrative and how you tell it matters a lot! Let me narrate an experiment done by the insurance company, MetLife. The research was conducted by Dr Martin Seligman who is well-known for his work on positive psychology.

'Every year, MetLife hires sales professionals. And every year, they hire the best ones they can find. At the time of conducting this experiment, Dr Seligman hired candidates who initially did not qualify to join. They were just below the cut-off line on a lot of skills and parametres. But he selected them because they were very high on optimism. He wanted to use them as a study group and had them put on the pay roll. As part of the experiment, they were sent out into the field and observed for two years.

'In the first year, the group selected by Dr Seligman outsold the people selected by MetLife by 21 per cent. In the second year, they outsold the MetLife guys by 57 per cent. Technically they had all failed the selection process, but they were selected for their optimism. So, what does this tell you?

'When we take a situation and bring our cognitive perspective to it, broadly speaking, there can be two extremes. One is pessimistic and the other is optimistic.

'The first thing a pessimist does is to make the situation personal. They tend to say, "I failed and I am such a failure." The optimist, on the other hand, says, "Okay, yeah, I didn't succeed this time. But it is based on several factors." They do not make the situation entirely personal.

'The other big difference is that the pessimist thinks this situation is permanent: "Because I did not close this deal, I think I will never close another deal in my life." The optimist understands that things happened a certain way because of certain reasons, and it was just a temporary setback. They have confidence they will close the next deal or the one after that.

'Finally, the last difference between a pessimist and an optimist is that of pervasiveness. The former thinks that because they didn't succeed in one area, they are a failure in all areas of life. The thought process could be something like, "Oh my God, I didn't close this sales deal. Maybe it means I'm no good. Maybe I'm not even a good human being!" They apply the feeling to all areas of life. The optimist sees it differently: "Hey, look, I failed in this instance. I didn't close this deal but that doesn't make me a loser. That doesn't make me a failure or a bad human being!" Intuitively, everybody likes an optimist.'

As Krish spoke, Sid was repeatedly practising mindful listening, focusing intently on the words, their rhythm and the subtle inflections in Krish's tone. He let each idea settle in his mind without judgment, noticing how the distinctions between pessimism and optimism resonated within him. With each pause, he allowed space for the meaning to deepen, his awareness anchored in the present moment. Every time his mind wandered, he gently guided it back.

When Krish finished speaking, Sid tapped his fingers lightly on his knee, his brow furrowed in thought. 'So it's not just about how we experience failure,' he mused, 'but about how we frame it in our minds—how we narrate the story of the incident to ourselves and others.' He glanced at Krish, a faint smile playing on his lips.

'Yes. And why are these elements important? It is because this is what helps us when we are being beaten down by life. When we are facing a challenge, a situation which is difficult, this narrative becomes really important.

'Nothing is permanent. Good times will change. There will be setbacks. The setbacks will pass too, and there will be good times again. A fluid, adaptive kind of resilience is the skill that serves you in both times.

The best kind of resilience is resilience + optimism + mindfulness.

'Mindfulness here helps you become aware of your negativity. Remember, we talked about negativity bias when we discussed self-compassion? We all have a tendency to remember that one critical thing that was said to us by somebody at some point, but we have forgotten the thousands of good things people have shared about us. Mindfulness helps in knowing that you have a negativity bias which makes you look at things in a negative way. And then bringing mindful awareness to it, you see how to move away from that negative narrative.

'When you start to bring mindfulness into the equation, you are also able to look at things as they are, not as you are. Mindfulness brings awareness and the element of reality. This allows for transformation based on your resilience and not on hope. Transformation based on hope is when you sit and pray that you will get lucky. Hope, as they say, is not a strategy. On the other hand, transformation brought about through awareness of your negativity bias and an understanding of reality is sustainable.

'So, the question my friend is, instead of merely hoping and praying for things to change, how can you add optimism and mindfulness to your inbuilt sense of resilience? Since you already have resilience, the aim becomes to add optimism and mindfulness to your resilience.

'Let's start to become a little more aware of what your natural inclination is. When you are self-aware, you learn what you need to fix. I will try to explain through a story.

> A man was stuck in the floods. He had to climb onto the rooftop of his house as the flood waters swirled around him. A devout man, he prayed to God to save him. A boat passed by and the people shouted to him to join them. 'No! God will save me!' he shouted back and went back to prayer. A little later a helicopter flew in his vicinity, dropping a ladder to the man. 'No! God will save me!' he shouted back. Eventually, the flood waters rose and the man drowned.
>
> In heaven, he met God. 'I was devout all my life. Why did you not save me when I needed you the most?' he asked. 'Well, I did send a boat first and then a helicopter to save you! It didn't look like you wanted to be saved,' God replied.

Sid burst into laughter as Krish ended with a smile. Both men sat in silence for a few minutes as Sid reflected on the story. Like all of Krish's stories, it hid a deeper meaning that revealed itself when you paused and looked for it.

'So, let's try a little exercise,' Krish resumed eventually. 'I am going to ask you to first think of a recent setback that you had, whether personal or professional. It could be a situation or circumstance when you did not meet expectations or your boss did not like the outcome. Close your eyes, take a few deep breaths and then breathe slowly, allowing your mind to settle.'

Sid was by now familiar with this process. As he allowed himself to shift into a different state, he started to recall the incident.

Sid had woken up that fateful morning to the familiar haze of exhaustion, his body sluggish, his mind a tangled web of pending tasks and unresolved emails. He swung his legs out of bed, intending to shuffle towards the bathroom, but as he stood, the world tilted. His vision blurred, his knees buckled, and before he could steady himself, he collapsed on the cold floor. For a few moments, he lay there, stunned and disoriented, his heart pounding in his chest. As he dragged himself to the bathroom, he wondered if he'd had a stroke or even a heart attack.

'Bring to mind details of this setback. Where were you when it happened? Who was involved? What was said or done that led to the setback? How did the people who were involved feel? And how did *you* feel? Was there a sense of guilt, disappointment, shame?'

At the hospital, the diagnosis was delivered with brutal clarity. Burnout. Complete and unrelenting. 'You need to stop,' the doctor had said, her tone firm and unsympathetic.

'Your body is demanding what you've denied it for years—rest.'

For the first time in as long as he could remember, Sid had no choice but to listen. He was forced to stay in the hospital for observation, tethered to monitors and a bed that felt more like a prison than a sanctuary. The sterile white walls seemed to mock him, each passing hour hammering home the futility of the hectic lifestyle he had adopted.

The nights were the hardest. Without the distraction of work, his thoughts swirled like a storm. He thought about the family dinners he had missed, the calls he had ignored, the moments of joy he had sacrificed on the altar of ambition. The weight of those realizations pressed down on him, making sleep elusive.

Where were you? Sid visualized the bathroom floor, the chill of the tiles against his skin, the overwhelming sense of helplessness.

Who was involved? His mind flashed to the worried faces of the paramedics, the concerned call from his mother, and the colleague who sent a terse email asking about the delayed report even as Sid lay in the hospital bed.

What was said or done? The doctor's voice echoed in his memory, harsh yet necessary: 'This isn't sustainable. You need to stop.'

How did you feel? Sid felt a knot in his stomach as he remembered the guilt, shame and crushing realization that he had brought this upon himself. His thoughts churned: *I should have known better. I'm supposed to be stronger. Why didn't I see this coming?*

One night, in particular, he stared at the ceiling, the faint hum of the machines his only companion. 'What am I doing with my life?' he had whispered into the darkness. The question lingered, unanswered, as the hours crawled by.

'Without judgement, just observe your emotions. Focus on them and feel them fully. Now, bring some curiosity and kind attention as you check in on your mental and emotional condition right now. Do you feel like you have a lot of thoughts and emotions? Is there a sort of dull, defeated feeling? How would you name the kind of thoughts you are having? Are they frustrating or depressing, worrying? Are you just replaying the incident? Are there thoughts like, "I was not good enough", "I am not good enough", "I should have known" or "I will never be able to get it right"? What kind of emotions are there under these thoughts? Can you put a label or a mental post-it on the emotions?' Krish's gentle yet powerful voice encouraged Sid to unwrap the mental and emotional state that the memory had stirred up.

'Is there something like a sinking feeling? There could even be something like determination. Take your awareness now to your body and notice how you are sitting. Has your posture changed? Are you slouching as you visualize the setback? Are your shoulders drooping? Has your head gone down? Without trying to change anything, just notice the body for any tightness or tension anywhere. Is there some tightness or tension in the neck, shoulders, upper back? How about the face? Is there any tension in the throat or the chest? Notice your breathing. Is it shallow or deep? Without changing anything, simply notice how your stomach feels.

'Stay with the emotions. Imagine that a good friend is sharing something difficult and you are waiting for them to finish before you say anything.'

Krish's instructions led Sid deeper into his self. He noticed the weight in his chest, the tightness in his shoulders, the shallow rhythm of his breathing. He labelled the emotions: guilt, regret, frustration. There was even a trace of anger—at himself, at the system that glorified burnout and at the choices he had made including the relentless pursuit of power and money.

'Now bring a gentle sense of kindness into that space, knowing that whatever you felt has also been experienced by many others. You are not alone. Remember that the emotion is not you; it is simply a phenomenon that you are observing. Just float in that awareness.'

As Krish prompted him to bring kindness into the space, Sid softened. He imagined talking to a friend in the same situation. *What would I tell them?* The answer was clear: *It's okay. You're human. This isn't the end, just a step in the journey.*

'Now, let us explore some possibilities for transformation. Try to see if you can give yourself a little bit of compassion and generosity. You are a human being. You too have setbacks and needs. Notice if you took this setback personally. Imagine if you were talking to a friend who has just experienced the same setback. What would you say to him or her? Would you tell them it's okay? Would you offer them a broader perspective of the situation?' Krish continued.

'Were you imagining your setback to be permanent? Consider instead what could happen after the setback. Consider the setback not as an enemy but just another step in a long journey. What are your values which you can rely on now to give you direction and strength? Take your awareness back to your thoughts. What kind of thoughts are going in your head? How are you narrating the situation to yourself? How does your body feel? Has your posture changed?'

As he followed Krish's guidance, Sid started to sense a change. Was this burnout a permanent mark on his life? Or was it a wake-up call, an opportunity to rebuild? He imagined the values he could lean on—resilience, balance, connection—and how they could guide him forward.

'Now, imagine that you have been successful in this situation. You have overcome this setback and succeeded. You exceeded expectations. What does that situation look like? Can you visualize that outcome? What are people saying? What are they doing? How do you feel? What emotions does this bring out now? Where do you notice changes again in the body? Has your posture changed? Sensations of success are pleasant so we want them to stay but just observe and play with them without getting attached. Experience all these things as they come and go. Emotions like success and failure come and go, like clouds in the big blue sky which is your life. It's all part of the journey.'

With each deep breath, Sid felt the tension in his body ease. His posture straightened and the knot in his stomach loosened. He imagined what success from here on would look like: a life where work and rest co-existed, where he felt energized, not drained, and where his relationships flourished alongside his career.

Sid saw himself thriving—mentoring his team, sharing dinners with loved ones, rediscovering his passion for painting. The emotions accompanying this vision were uplifting: joy, pride, hope. His shoulders squared, his chest expanded and a faint smile now played on his lips.

'Taking your awareness to your breath, let go of all these memories and emotions. Notice the movement of the chest, notice your body, your mind and your feelings. Whenever you are ready, just open your eyes and come back. Take a deep breath. Let go of this whole memory and just set it aside,' said Krish as he concluded the exercise.

As he opened his eyes, Sid felt lighter, as though he had shed a heavy burden. The journey wasn't over, but for the first time in years, he felt equipped to take the next step—not by pushing harder, but by moving mindfully, one moment at a time. Wordlessly he stood up, stepped across to Krish and hugged him. Krish gently patted Sid on the back and held him. Sid felt goosebumps. It was almost like he had just plugged into a charging station.

'Thank you!' was all he could bring himself to say in that moment as he slowly let go of Krish.

'There is a wonderful quality that mindfulness brings about. If you remember, I said there are three things to this kind of resilience—inner calm, emotional resilience and cognitive resilience.

'When there is inner calm, there is greater clarity. There is a word "equanimity" that describes emotional resilience. Equanimity means you are calm and composed with your emotions, no matter what happens. When you look at what your experience was, just explore a few aspects for yourself. What was your narrative style? Was it optimistic or pessimistic? Just observing these patterns starts to build your awareness and thereby your resilience.'

Krish then guided Sid further by sharing some more techniques to build resilience.

Day 7: Bend, Not Break: A Fluid Quality of Resilience 179

1. *Having a Sense of Belonging*: This can be done in different ways. You could belong to a team. We see this in sports. Belonging to a team allows you to bounce back in a good way. Being a part of a team, a department, an effort, a company, a group, a family, and at some level, a part of humanity. Belonging to something larger than yourself tells you that you are not alone. It is a very strong factor in building your resilience.
2. *A Meaningful Life*: We discussed this when we spoke about motivation. You can have a pleasant life, but it doesn't last very long and it can change quite frequently. It's like eating an ice-cream; the first one is really good, the second one is good, sort of, the third one is okay. After the fourth, you don't want any more ice-cream. A meaningful life is one of engagement; it uses all our skills and strengths. It is a life which has a purpose larger than ourselves.
3. *Giving Up Control*: Just know that there are many things one doesn't understand and one cannot control. Some people call it God, some people refer to it as a spiritual dimension—the choice is yours. Just understand that there are things at play which are much larger than you and I. We live on a planet in a solar system with many planets. The solar system is one of many such systems in the Milky Way and the Milky Way is one of many such galaxies. You are one tiny, little human being in all this. Even just bringing in this perspective helps!
4. *Humour*: Life is too important to be taken seriously. Humour is a crucial, interesting aspect of resilience. Just being able to laugh at a situation and say, 'That is

so funny, I should have said that and done that but this is what happened.' Looking at life in a humorous way, looking at yourself in a humorous way, allows you to take the punches when they come.

5. *Creativity*: Creativity and mindfulness are very close friends. One fuels the other and interestingly, both of them fuel resilience. So in difficult situations, how can you be more creative? How can you be more innovative?
6. *Adaptability*: The creatures that survive extreme unpredictability and evolve are not the most physically strong creatures. If that were true, dinosaurs would still be around. Even the most intelligent of creatures don't necessarily survive. The ones who survive are the ones who can adapt. So, equip yourself to be flexible, nimble, agile and not get stuck. Just go with the flow, go with the Tao as they say in Taoism.
7. *Ability to Identify Resources*: What do you have right now? What can you leverage? How can you be creative about it? How can you brainstorm and come up with new ideas? When the mind is busy and scared, you might not even be able to think of the resources that you have. So, calm down and check your resource box again!
8. *Cheerleader*s: Last, but not the least, have your own cheerleaders. Who is that buddy who reminds you that you are not too bad? Who can remind you of your past successes? Who can remind you that you are actually quite capable? Have them on speed dial.

'Those are some of the best tools you could add to your resilience kit,' Krish finally concluded.

Day 7: Bend, Not Break: A Fluid Quality of Resilience

Sid leaned back against the pillar of the veranda, his hand brushing gently over the wood as he grounded himself with the help of the texture.

'You know, Krish, everything you just said makes so much sense,' he began, his voice tinged with awe. 'It's fascinating how resilience isn't just about toughening up—it's about lightening up, too. Humour, belonging, creativity . . . these are things I never thought of as tools for bouncing back.'

He paused, his gaze drifting to a cluster of wildflowers swaying gently in the breeze. 'I guess I've been too focused on just powering through challenges, thinking sheer grit was enough. But now, I can see how it's about finding balance, staying adaptive and leaning into the resources and people around you.'

Krish smiled knowingly, sensing Sid's deep engagement. 'Exactly, Sid. Resilience isn't a solo journey—it's about how you navigate challenges with awareness, adaptability and a touch of lightness.'

Sid chuckled softly, shaking his head. 'It's funny how often we complicate things when the answers can be so simple. But I'm curious—what happens when everything seems stacked against you? When even resilience feels impossible?' Krish had that twinkle in his eye that suggested he was ready with another suitable story.

Donkeys, as you know, are very resilient creatures. This donkey had served its master, a farmer, for many, many years. But eventually, like all things, this donkey aged. It was no longer able to lift a heavy load and be productive. So, the farmer was a little tired of the donkey. One day, when the donkey was roaming around in the fields, it fell into a well. Fortunately, the well was dry, but it couldn't come out. So, it started braying from inside the well.

The farmer heard it and went to look. He saw the donkey at the bottom of the well. He said to himself, 'Maybe he has served his purpose. Maybe it's time I help him pass on to the next life.' He called other farmers from nearby and asked them to come with spades. He said to them, 'Look, my donkey, old chap, has fallen into the well. Let's help him pass on to the next world.' So, the farmers all started digging the earth outside and throwing the mud into the well.

The donkey was terrified initially—he realized what was happening. His master was going to bury him. He started braying more loudly. The farmers ignored it and went on pouring more and more mud into the well. Soon, the sound stopped. The farmers continued. After some time, when they checked, they were really surprised. The old donkey was shaking off the mud falling on him and had constantly been climbing on it. That's why he had stopped braying. In fact, he was quite happy because he was almost in a position to climb out of the well.

'Isn't that a great example of how to leverage your resources in a difficult moment to come out of a setback?' Krish asked, finishing the story.

'It certainly is!' said Sid. 'I have been thinking and I had a question. What is the difference between optimism and positive thinking?'

'Good question!' said Krish. 'Optimism is a belief in positive outcomes while positive thinking is a deliberate, present-moment practice of focusing on the good aspects of a situation. Think of it like this. Optimism is a trait and positive thinking is a mindset. Both skills can be trained!'

> **When you feel attached, tell it to the fire. He is great at transmuting states.**
> **When you feel stagnant, talk to the water. She knows about movement and flow and doesn't hold on to anything.**
> **When you understand nothing, speak to the wind. It will bring you to the here and now and clarity will come to your soul.**
> **When you want to give up, talk to Mother Earth. She knows about rebirths.**
> **When you feel that life overwhelms you, talk to the plants. They are the guardians of patience and growth.**
> **When you feel you can't take it anymore, talk to the stars. Their light will remind you that even if the path is dark, there's always a ray of hope.**
> **When you feel like you have lost your way, talk to the mountains. They are eternal witnesses of perseverance and stability.**
> **When you feel your heart is broken, talk to the Moon. She knows about cycles and will remind you that you can always shine again. Even after the darkness.**

Sid nodded slowly, absorbing the words. He patted the floor at his side, as though grounding himself in the present moment. 'So, it's not just about bouncing back—it's about transforming through the experience,' he murmured, a glimmer of understanding crossing his face.

Krish smiled and leaned forward slightly, his tone shifting. 'Nature is one of the most beautiful and powerful metaphors for resilience. Let me tell you another story.

> Two travelling monks came to a river they had to cross, but the river was in spate. It had rained a lot so it was flowing heavily and they couldn't walk across. On the bank of the river, there was a young woman who was crying because she had to go home. She wanted to go to the other side, so without thinking too much, one of the monks offered to help her. He picked her up and they swam across the river. Reaching the other side, he set the woman down and the monks continued on their path. One of the monks was really upset. After two hours, he asked, 'How could you do that? You are a monk; you are not supposed to touch a woman and yet you went ahead and did that.' The monk who helped the girl said, 'I did that but I also left her on the river bank after we reached the other side. Why are you still carrying her?'

'So, many times, pain and suffering are created because of our response and the fact that we carry so much baggage with us.' As Krish finished the story, he leaned back with a serene smile, letting the wisdom of the tale settle in the air between them. Sid sat quietly, absorbing the lesson. The sun cast its shadows across the veranda.

Sid broke the silence, his voice soft yet thoughtful. 'It's incredible how much baggage we carry without even realizing it. I wonder how often I've been like that monk, holding onto something I should've left behind.'

Krish nodded knowingly. 'It happens to all of us, Sid. But the key is awareness. Once you notice the weight, you can choose to set it down.'

> **Try not to resist the changes that come.**
> **Go with the flow.**
> **Let life flow through you.**
> **And when life seems to have turned upside down,**
> **remember that this side may well be better than the**
> **side you were used to!**

Krish stood up, brushing off his jeans, and glanced towards the pathway leading to the farm's exit. 'Sid, I need to step out for a while. There's something I need to attend to in the village.' He turned to Sid with a warm smile. 'Why don't you take some rest? Or, if you feel like it, take a walk in the neighbourhood around the farm. It's a good place to reflect—plenty of quiet corners to sit and let your thoughts breathe.'

Sid nodded, a small smile playing on his lips. 'That sounds like a good idea, Krish. Thanks.'

As Krish disappeared down the pathway, Sid continued to enjoy the quiet settling around him like a comforting blanket. The thought of a short nap was almost irresistible and he decided to head back to his room. The rustle of the leaves outside his window soon hushed him into a light, restful sleep.

The late afternoon sun flickered on the wall as Sid awoke feeling fresh and energized. He decided to take Krish's suggestion and walk around the farm. The crisp air was laced with the fragrance of flowers and felt invigorating. Sid walked past rows of vegetables and fruit trees deeply inhaling the scent of freshly tilled soil and soaking in the peace of the surroundings.

As he neared an open field, he spotted a young boy clutching a bright red kite. The boy was frowning in concentration, struggling to get the kite airborne. The kite flapped before crashing repeatedly to the ground. Sid chuckled softly and walked over.

'Need some help?' he asked.

The boy looked up, eyes lighting up at the offer. 'Yes, please! It just won't fly.'

Sid picked up the kite, inspecting its frame and thread. 'Alright, let's give it another go.'

Together, they positioned the kite against the wind. Sid guided the boy on when to release the thread and when to pull it taut. With a running start, the kite began to lift, wobbling before catching the breeze. It soared higher and higher, the boy whooping with delight.

Sid held the thread for a moment, feeling its gentle tug. As the kite danced in the sky, a thought struck him. The resistance of the wind—the very force pushing against it—was what allowed the kite to rise. Without the tension of the thread anchoring it to the ground, the kite would likely drift away aimlessly. It was the interplay of these opposing forces—resistance and anchoring—that allowed the kite to soar.

Sid's grip on the thread tightened as an 'aha' moment washed over him. *Isn't this what resilience is all about?* he thought. The wind represents challenges and resistance, things that push against us. The thread is our anchor—our values, purpose and awareness—keeping us grounded. It's not about avoiding the wind or cutting loose from the thread. It's about balancing the two forces, using them together to rise high in the sky.

He handed the thread back to the boy, smiling. 'You've got it now. Keep it steady.'

As the boy took over, Sid stood watching the kite climb even higher, the interplay of forces now a vivid metaphor in his mind. He felt a sense of clarity, a quiet understanding of how challenges could be turned into opportunities for growth. Life, like the kite, wasn't about avoiding resistance or letting go of anchors—it was about finding strength in the balance.

As the boy's laughter echoed across the field, Sid gave him a thumbs-up and began making his way back to the farm. The kite's graceful dance against the sky lingered in his thoughts, each loop and dive reinforcing the insight he had just uncovered. The sun was beginning to dip below the horizon, painting the farm in hues of amber and rose, and a gentle breeze carried the soft rustle of leaves.

Reaching his room, Sid kicked off his shoes and sat at the wooden desk by the window. The bamboo tree just outside bent with the wind. *I will bend. But not break. And what does not break me, will only make me stronger and wiser.* It seemed to be respectfully bowing and saying to the strong wind that was howling through the trees today.

As he opened his journal to a fresh page, the possibilities of a blank page greeted him. With a deep breath, he took up his pen and began to write.

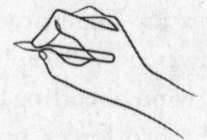

While I envision and manifest my, life there are sure to be challenges and setbacks that test me.

I can use these setbacks and challenges to build the skills which, when the setbacks or challenges have passed, become my superpowers and allow me to thrive not just survive.

This kind of resilience comes out of developing deep emotional resilience or equanimity and developing a positive and optimistic narrative of the setback itself.

I can see how it's about finding balance, staying adaptive, and leaning into the resources and people around you.

Optimism is a trait and positive thinking is more of a mindset. Both skills can be trained!

As I bring my mindfulness to bear on all these elements and give myself a bit of self-compassion, like I would to a friend who had experienced a

> similar setback, I open myself up to the possibility of transformation.
>
> I want to live a life which has a purpose larger than my own.
>
> **My little practice:**
>
> Stop. Breathe. Check my narrative. Proceed.
>
> **Reflection questions:**
>
> What is the one problem in my life that has given me the greatest growth?
>
> Who can I enlist as my cheerleader?

Sid placed the pen down, a faint smile on his face. Closing the journal, he leaned back, letting the day's learnings settle in. The kite's dance played in his mind one last time as the cool evening air filtered through the window. With a quiet resolve, he promised himself to hold on to today's lessons and explore them further tomorrow.

Part 3

Leading Others and Bringing Out the Best in Them

Day 8: Empathy and Building Great Teams

The next morning, Sid found Krish putting a few things into a bag. It looked like he was preparing to head out somewhere.

'Good morning, my friend!' he called out cheerfully. 'I'm just heading to a nearby farm to pick up some supplies. Would you like to come along?' he asked.

Sid did not want to miss out on a single moment of self-reflection with Krish.

'Of course! I'd love that. Is there anything I can do to help?' he asked Krish enthusiastically. It was remarkable how Sid's energy had changed ever since he had come to this place. In the few days he had been there, he felt lighter, energized and happier. There was an underlying sense of calm and clarity. Sid had wondered on more than one occasion if it was because there was some magic in the fresh air or some elixir in the food he was being given. Or simply, just the magnetic presence of this man.

'Here! Grab this while I get the keys to the truck,' said Krish as he threw a light duffel bag at Sid.

A few minutes later, they were in the truck and heading onto a winding road. The scenery was beautiful. A slight mist swirled through the trees on either side of the road as Bono sang 'Where The Streets Have No Name' through the speakers of the truck.

Both men drove in silence, almost as if they had an unspoken understanding that to speak would do injustice to the moment. A short drive later they arrived at a large gate. Wire fences extended on both sides of the gate. On the gate, a sign said: 'PUPPIES FOR SALE!'

As Sid and Krish got out of the car, they saw a little boy standing near the gate trying to look through the gaps in the gate. On the other side, a man was approaching.

'That's my farmer friend,' Krish said to Sid as he waved to the man.

'Good morning, Krish sir! I saw your truck coming and came up to receive you. Welcome!' he said as he opened the gate. It was then that the man noticed the little boy.

'Who are you, little chap, and what do you want?' he asked the boy.

'Sir, I saw your notice that you have puppies for sale. Im here to buy one for myself.'

'Okay' young man! But I need to tell you that my dog is a very special dog. It's a pedigree and the puppies are therefore expensive because they are a very good breed.' The farmer was quite amused as he realized the boy was there alone.

Day 8: Empathy and Building Great Teams

The little boy said, 'Sure' sir. I understand. Which is why I brought my entire piggybank. I will give you everything that I have in this.'

The farmer looked at Krish and smiled. The men knew that the coins in the piggybank were not enough to buy a puppy. But it was clear that the farmer didn't have the heart to say 'no' to the little boy. He decided to indulge the little boy and opened the gate. He said, 'OK, come in everybody,' and as they entered, he whistled sharply.

Hearing the whistle, the farmer's dog came bounding out of her kennel. Four little balls of fur followed her. The boy looked at them and was thrilled. And then slowly, from the kennel, another fifth ball of fur emerged. And this puppy was coming much more slowly. It was not bouncing along as fast as the other puppies.

As the dog and the pups reached the little group, it became apparent that the fifth puppy was slow because it had a deformed leg.

The men watched the boy in silence as he looked at the dogs with absolute delight on his face.

After a few moments of silence, the boy looked at the farmer and held out his piggybank.

'Sir, take my money, and I will take that puppy,' he said pointing to the fifth one.

Krish turned to look at Sid with a smile as if to say that he had expected this. Sid had not expected this.

The farmer seemed as surprised as Sid. 'No, my son. You don't want to take that puppy, because that puppy is lame. He cannot walk or run very well.'

The little boy looked up at the farmer, pulled up the right leg of his pants and showed his leg. He had a brace. He said,

'Sir, I have a lame leg myself and I cannot walk or run very fast. So, I think I would really like that little fellow because we will understand each other.'

Sid's eyes welled up when he heard this. The farmer sat next to the boy. He gently pushed the piggybank back in his hands. He then stood up and went across to the pups who were playing, picked up the little lame pup and brought it to the boy.

'Here.' He said. 'He's yours. Use the money to buy some treats.'

The boy could not believe his ears. He hugged the farmer's leg. 'Thank you!' he said as he then opened his arms to receive his new friend.

'Okay. Off you go now! I have work to do!' The farmer waved to Krish and Sid to follow him to the farmhouse.

They left an hour later, after Krish had collected a bag of fruits and vegetables. Sid had been quiet all along, leaving Krish and his friend to their conversation. The incident with the little boy had touched a chord deep inside him.

'I'd like to ask you something. How would you explain the incident we witnessed back there with the lame puppy and the little boy?' Sid said to Krish a few minutes after they had left.

'Would it be alright if I responded to you once we got back?' asked Krish. 'I just want to enjoy listening to the wind blow.'

When they reached, Krish said he was going to put away the fruits and vegetables.

Sid though was still replaying the poignant moment between the boy and the lame puppy. It had left him restless, a stirring he couldn't quite place.

Day 8: Empathy and Building Great Teams

Later, he emerged from his room, hoping to spot Krish.

As he walked around the open spaces, he found Krish sitting on the wooden bench by the lotus pond, his posture relaxed, his gaze distant yet grounded. Sid hesitated for a moment, then made his way towards him.

'Hello, Sid!' Krish called out when he saw him approaching. 'Want to join me?'

'What are you doing?' asked Sid as he couldn't really see Krish doing anything.

'I'm watching the lotus bloom! And in that process, I'm just being. Would you like to join me in that? Just being a human being for a while instead of a human doing!' he laughed as Sid went and sat next to him.

'When you put it like that, I don't know if I have ever really been a human being!' laughed Sid. 'So yes, I'd love to just be! And see what that feels like.'

'Wonderful. In that case, allow me to guide you with a few easy instructions. Start by just noticing your surroundings. With your eyes open, just notice where you are sitting. Observe what is around you, the trees, the colours, the textures. Simply allow your awareness to fill up with the sensation of sight. Take your entire awareness to the things you see.' Krish paused here for a few minutes to let Sid start soaking in his new experience.

As Sid settled into a comfortable posture, he let his gaze wander around. He saw a bird on a nearby tree. The colours of blue and green in its feathers were striking. The wooden bench under him seemed to support him with its rough presence. His breathing slowed further as he took in the colours of the plants, the different hues on the ground. There was a faint rustle of leaves and an earthy scent on the breeze. In the pond, the lotus bud had bloomed further.

'At some point, gently close your eyes,' Krish continued after a few minutes. 'Become aware of your body. Notice your posture. Notice your feet on the ground, the weight of the body on the bench, your arms placed on your legs. Explore the sensation of touch, the contact with the bench, the feeling of the fabric, maybe even the touch of the gentle breeze on your skin.' Krish again paused for a while for Sid to fill his awareness with these sensations.

'Now, take your awareness to the sounds around you—the sound of my voice and any other sounds you can hear,' Krish said after a few incredibly calm minutes.

Sid felt the endless mental chatter in his head slow down as he became more alert to the sounds around him. He heard the faraway cry of a kite or an eagle, some parrots screeching closer by.

'Now let us simply sit here. Not thinking of anything. Not doing anything. Just *being*. Because right now, there is nowhere else to be, but here. And nothing else to do.'

As Sid gave in to the mesmerizing voice guiding him, he felt a sense of awareness. A sense of being awake, conscious and alert. But without thought. It was almost as though he was the clear blue sky and the clouds had all blown away.

'Whenever you feel ready, take a few deep breaths and gently open your eyes,' Krish continued.

Time seemed to slow down and wait for Sid to return to the present moment. His eyes flickered as if unwilling to let go of the profound stillness he had found in closing them. As he slowly opened his eyes, the world around him seemed sharper. The colours brighter. The chirping clearer. And even the gentle breeze felt like it was embracing him.

Sid glanced at Krish, who sat still, his gaze steady but serene. They exchanged a quiet smile, both fully immersed in the tranquil space they had created. For a long time, neither of them spoke, the silence feeling more profound than any words could.

It was many minutes later that Sid eventually broke the silence. 'If this is what *being* is, I must definitely admit that I have come nowhere close to it!'

'Hmmm. Just recharging yourself by being is a great way of living,' Krish responded. 'Doing is important. Everything that we have created requires doing. However if you see properly, you realize that all creation comes from the purity of being. When we just *be*, we allow our body and mind to rest and recharge.

'Many times, I imagine myself simply sitting in a space just behind a waterfall. For me, the screen of water symbolises the separation between doing and being. As I rest in the space of being, I am awake, aware and conscious. But when the need to do something arises, I step out of the space, through the curtain of water, to *do*. I am then operating with the drops of consciousness still on me. If I move too far away from the waterfall, the drops of consciousness evaporate and I could then completely lose myself in mindless doing. So, when I sense the danger of this happening I choose to go back to replenish myself in the space of being.'

'I see what you mean, Krish. Right now, I feel my mind is calm and quiet. I can see things with a certain clarity and perspective I have not experienced before. I can imagine what it would be like for me to engage in any task right now. I think I would be able to bring a new level of engagement and quality to it,' Sid said.

'And the mental image of the waterfall with a space just behind the curtain of water is so beautiful. Such a powerful image,' continued Sid with his eyes now closed. 'I can almost see myself resting in *being* and then spacing it with very productive periods of *doing*. In my mind, it's like the energy of *being* is a sort of sticky glue that adds tremendous value to my activities. If I move too far away from the source of the glue, the connections could snap. Being aware, I need to ensure that this glue is always binding my conscious state with my actions!'

'This is very good, Sid. You certainly are learning fast,' said Krish after a few moments. It was probably the first time that he had directly complimented Sid, and its effect was not lost.

Sid felt a moment of pride at receiving this rare compliment from Krish. The words 'glue of being' reverberated in his mind as he leaned back on the bench. The two threads of *being* and *doing* looked clearer. Their interplay felt like something he could weave with awareness to create the beautiful tapestry of his life.

Krish observed Sid silently, his calm demeanour revealing just a hint of amusement. After a few moments, he leaned forward slightly, breaking the peaceful pause.

'Would you like to explore the incident this morning? The boy and the puppy?' asked Krish.

'Oh yes! I would love to. It was such a beautiful experience for me and I would love to learn from your perspective of it,' said Sid enthusiastically.

'Great timing of the incident if you ask me,' said Krish with a smile. Sid had by now learnt that this smile usually meant that Krish was going to elegantly unwrap something rather complex.

'We have discussed many aspects about ourselves till now. We looked inward, we talked of self-awareness, we understood our emotions and we gave ourselves more love through self-compassion. You even started to understand your values and motivations, how you can envision your life and build your resilience. Now, with the benefit of all that, let's look at what happened with the boy this morning.'

'Absolutely!' replied Sid. 'I think he felt a strong sense of connection to the lame puppy. He probably felt sorry for it because he knew what it must be like to have a disability. So, he could empathize with the puppy.'

'True. The boy certainly demonstrated some incredible qualities. But I actually see empathy a bit differently, Sid,' replied Krish. 'I think empathy is a bit like self-awareness. A lot of people think they have it, but the reality might be a little different.

'We use the word liberally—*I have a lot of empathy, that person has absolutely no empathy*, and so on and so forth. But what exactly does empathy mean? Empathy could be defined in two parts. The first is simple—it is the ability to experience and understand what others feel. This is relatively easy to understand. The second part is however perhaps much more important. It requires that you have an awareness about your own and the other person's feelings as well as perspectives, keeping in mind that they might be different.'

Sid tilted his head slightly, his brows knitting in curiosity. 'That's an interesting way to put it . . . How do you mean that?' asked Sid.

'That means you are able to understand what the other person is feeling, but it may or may not be your own perspective. You may or may not agree with them, yet, you understand that someone is feeling a certain way.

'Let me ask you to reflect on this. If someone is struggling and they share their pain with us, how often do we end up telling them that they should not be feeling that way? Sometimes we also respond by saying that we have a similar or a larger problem as if that is going to make them feel any better. How often have we seen this or how often have we done this ourselves?'

'Oh, I am guilty of doing both of these things quite regularly myself,' Sid confessed almost immediately. He could see it now.

An incident came to his mind immediately. Aditi had shared that sometimes she felt hurt at the casual way Sid would speak of his past relationships. While she knew it was from his past and nothing could change, it did make her feel a certain way. She was being vulnerable and transparent as she shared her deepest feelings. Sid almost winced as his poor reaction flashed across his mind.

'There's no reason for you to feel that way. My past is my past and I'm done trying to explain that to you. Neither of us can change anything. I suggest you stop feeling like that!' he had said. And as if that was not bad enough, 'There are things from your past too that don't feel great for me! I deal with it, right?'

He remembered Aditi going quiet. After a while, the conversation moved on to other things. As he looked back, Sid couldn't help but wish that he had responded differently.

Krish watched Sid's obvious discomfort at the memories in his mind and sat in silence, waiting for him to settle. Sid closed his eyes and took a few deep breaths.

'To understand this further, let's see what empathy is not. First of all, it is not sympathy. The root for all these words is "pathy", which means "to feel",' he resumed after he sensed that Sid was feeling better. 'These words are often used interchangeably. Empathy is definitely not the same as sympathy. Sympathy is when you feel pity for someone.

'"I sympathize with your pain," does not mean you are sharing their pain. It suggests talking from a place where that pain doesn't exist! You're not feeling their pain; you are in a better position, so you can afford to sympathize. You feel sympathetic towards a homeless person. You feel sympathetic towards a poor person, towards somebody who is injured or has cancer. But you are not in that position yourself. Do you know, researchers have found that patients receiving sympathy describe it as superficial and unwanted although well-intended?

'Think of a spectrum of these emotions. On the negative end of the spectrum are apathy and antipathy which denote negative feelings. Again, "pathy" remains constant. "Apathy" is probably somewhere towards the middle, where you have no feelings—you just don't care. Then you have sympathy, where you have pity for the feelings or situation of another. And then you have empathy, where you understand the feelings of that person even though you may not necessarily share them. And finally comes compassion.

'Now, these differences are important. In your personal as well as professional life. As a leader, you need to remember that empathy is not about wearing the hat of a psychologist and being a counsellor to somebody or trying to solve someone's problems. That is not empathy. Empathy is also not about agreeing with people.'

Sid nodded slowly, his fingers tapping thoughtfully on the edge of the bench. 'I can see why it's such an important skill, especially for a leader. It's not about fixing things for someone but about being present enough to truly understand their experience.'

Krish smiled, clearly pleased. 'Exactly, Sid. Let me explain further with an example.'

One day, a close friend of mine called me up and said, 'Hey, buddy, can I come and meet you? I'm in really bad shape.' I said, 'Well, sure. What happened?' So, he said, 'I'll explain, let me just come and meet you.' So, I said, 'OK, do come.'

He worked at a large IT company. He told me he had been working extremely hard for quite some time towards a promotion. He was very sure he was going to get it. He thought he had done everything and deserved the promotion. He had convinced himself that it was in the bag.

On the day of the appraisal, he was really upset to hear that he hadn't been promoted. When he came to see me, he told me how his boss had been unfair. He believed that the company, system and the whole world was against him.

Many people would have either agreed or disagreed. People in that moment would have said, 'Yeah, yeah,

Day 8: Empathy and Building Great Teams

I know your boss. He's terrible,' just to make the friend feel better. Or somebody else might have said, 'You know what, I told you this long back—the whole problem is with you!'

They would have played the role of a psychologist. They would have said, 'You know, this problem goes back to this', or 'It's your karma'. According to me, that is not empathy. Empathy starts when you really listen to the other person.

In this scenario, my friend was clearly upset. A lot of the time, I just said, 'Hmm!', 'I see', 'Okay', 'Aha' and allowed him to speak and vent out his thoughts and feelings. After about forty-five minutes, when he had finished, he said, 'Thank you for listening to me, I'll carry on now. You also have work to do. I'll catch up with you later.' He was already visibly feeling better. I just gave him a hug and sent him on his way.

After a couple of days, I called him up and I asked, 'Hey, how are you doing? Do you want to meet?' So he said, 'Yeah, sure. I'll drop by in the evening.' That evening I said, 'Look, in my opinion, here's what you could have done better. Had you done this, this, this, maybe you would have actually got the promotion that you were looking for.' And because he was calmer and had put some distance between himself and the event, he was able to accept the advice and understand it in a very positive way.

In the first instance, empathy from me was to understand that he was upset and just be there. I didn't agree with his reasoning, I didn't think his boss was a bad guy. In fact, I knew the boss too and I thought he was good. But that was not the time to tell him. Empathy is sometimes just about being there, and not offering any advice, opinion or suggestion.

'I understand. So can one actually develop this quality? I thought it was innate,' said Sid

'Empathy can be learnt,' said Krish, 'through certain practices of seeing similarities between ourselves and others.'

'But before we go there, I would like you to understand that there are a few different levels to empathy. At one level, there is cognitive empathy. That means that at a mental level, you are able to understand what the other person might be going through. Your rational mind is able to see that situation and understand what happened and that it could have potentially felt a certain way for them.

'The next level of empathy is more emotional. This is where you are able to understand the feelings of another person. You may or may not feel the same way but you are able to resonate with their feelings. This is a level where a great deal of awareness is required. Because otherwise, you can end up with empathic distress—a state where you start to feel the pain of the other person and it starts to impact you. Do you know that caregivers are the most likely to suffer from empathic distress? They are constantly dealing with patients who are in pain and suffering, and sometimes it gets overwhelming for them. Finally, at another level, there is a sense of wanting to know what could help the other person.

'There are several models of empathy and even more theories. But for me, a few simple attributes stand out. Firstly, what does that concept or experience mean or look like for you? Secondly, non-judgemental listening.

Day 8: Empathy and Building Great Teams

Thirdly, understanding the other person's emotion even if by asking questions. And lastly, letting them know we are understanding their emotion or that we are not—"Damn! I can't even imagine how hard that must've felt!" is okay too.'

Sid leaned back slightly, his expression thoughtful as he processed Krish's explanation. 'I can see how these levels of empathy—cognitive, emotional and supportive—can be game-changers, especially when combined with awareness.'

He couldn't help but think how he could have responded differently to Aditi. 'I understand cognitively that this aspect of my life might be difficult for you. Although I cannot change anything from the past, I'd like to understand better what kind of feelings you have.'

And as he reflected in this manner, Sid started to realize that even though he may not have felt the same kind of or degree of emotions as Aditi, the way she felt was not 'wrong' for her. It was her reality.

Krish nodded with a smile, sensing Sid's growing clarity. 'Exactly, Sid. And to build on that, let me also tell you how empathy shapes the dynamics not just between two individuals but also of teams and large groups.

'Google, which has thousands of people, studied teams across the globe to see what made for a perfect team or a high-performance team. Of course, there were all the usual aspects—clear vision, great delegation, excellent communication, structure, systems. But they still could not find one common factor among all the great teams. They analysed many teams, until finally, they discovered something very interesting.

'Structure, clarity, dependability, impact, vision are all important, but the most important factor is psychological safety which is nothing but empathy. A team where people are not out to take each other's roles or take away credit from somebody else is one that is high on empathy. An empathetic team is one where everybody feels connected, heard, understood and behaves as if they are completely supported. They are not afraid to take risks and they are not afraid to fail because they know that they will be supported.

'I'll give you another radically different case—tactical warfare. Imagine soldiers practising mindfulness and building empathy because what it takes to be really successful in a tactical warfare unit is not just strength and speed. The cost of training a high-performance soldier is high. After years of training, some of these people are selected for specialized tactical units. Once there, they undergo more training. By the time they finally get assigned, they are probably worth a lot in terms of training costs. They then go into extremely high-stress situations for high-precision operations.

'When they enter a building that is under threat, and the soldier in front looks to the right, the one behind them looks to the left. They are wired to take care of each other. And that is how they survive. That is how they make these highly risky operations so successful. Because of their ability to take care of each other. If the armed forces are using mindfulness to build empathy, you can imagine the kind of impact that mindfulness can have for building high-performance teams in the corporate world.

'In the corporate world, when managers take their teams out for a meal or an off-site, they are trying to build togetherness, empathy. They want people to be open and speak freely. In fact, as a leader, this is a skill you really want to develop.'

Sid leaned forward, his gaze steady as he absorbed Krish's words. 'So, if I'm hearing this right,' he began thoughtfully, 'empathy isn't just about individual understanding—it's also the glue that holds teams together. Whether it's in a corporate setup or even in something as high-stakes as a tactical unit, the ability to trust, support and look out for one another makes all the difference. It's not just a soft skill; it's a survival skill.'

Krish smiled, again sensing Sid's growing understanding. 'Exactly, Sid. And building that kind of empathetic environment starts with recognizing the importance of social connections within the team. That means that the people in a team also need to have social connections with each other. It's not just about finishing what needs to be done that day. They need to have a social bond. They need to be looking out for each other.

'The other important thing is an environment at work where each person can speak equally and freely. Nobody should feel afraid to speak or say anything. When there is psychological safety, people don't fear negative consequences. They're not afraid to try something, because even if they are challenged or fail, their team will support them.

'According to a study conducted by Gallup, employees who are taken care of feel ten times more than anybody else that their company or team is a great place to work. They are nine times more likely to stay in their company for a long time and make a great contribution, seven times more likely to feel included at work and four times less likely to suffer from stress and burnout. They are also twice as likely to be more productive and more engaged at work.

'Empathy, on the other hand, is also easily affected by certain factors. For example, if I feel that I'm being treated unfairly at any point in time, I'm not going to feel very empathetic towards the team. Or if the leader of the team treats me unfairly, I am not going to feel that much empathy towards that leader or even towards the team. So, fairness is really important. We all need to feel that there is a sense of fair play. Otherwise, the level of empathy drops. Then we don't care. Then apathy sets in and may even progress to antipathy.

'The second thing that affects empathy is a perception of "this is my team" and "that is somebody else's team". There is a fascinating experiment done by neuroscientist David Eagleman where people were taken into a lab and their brain was hooked up to a monitor which could show you which part of the brain is being activated. First, they were shown an image of a hand being stabbed. Even if you stop for a moment and imagine a picture of a hand being stabbed, what happens to you? You feel something, right? You shudder or close your eyes. That is empathy. Because when we see somebody as hurt or suffering, we also feel that pain. This is the fundamental law of nature. Human beings are wired to be empathetic.

'In the same study, researchers put a label next to the hand that was getting stabbed. The label was Muslim, Christian, Jew or Black. The result was shocking. If the hand did not belong to the observer's ethnicity, the pain they felt was much less. That means that if I'm Black, and I see a Black hand getting stabbed, I feel that pain but if I see a White hand getting stabbed, the pain I feel is much less. So, empathy is highly impacted both by perceived fairness and whether we feel the other person is part of our group or not.'

Sid leaned forward again, his elbows resting on his knees as he spoke, his voice reflective. 'Wow! That study you mentioned . . . it's unsettling to think how easily our empathy can be influenced. And we're doing it all the time from a very early age. We create differentiation. My religion versus yours. My country versus yours. My political party versus yours. My team versus yours.' He looked up at Krish, his gaze intent. 'But there's got to be a way to rise above that, right? To ensure we don't let those invisible barriers hold us back?'

Krish's eyes lit up as he nodded. 'There is, Sid. And the answer lies closer than you think—in the practice of self-awareness. Let me show you how it works. In fact, the same part of the brain is responsible for empathy as well as self-awareness, which means that practising self-awareness can actually induce more empathy!'

Krish leaned back slightly, his tone shifting to one of gentle guidance. 'Let's explore this connection together.' Sid adjusted his posture, sensing the shift in the conversation. He nodded, ready to follow Krish's lead.

'To gain from this synergy, we're going to activate some very specific parts of our brain. I want you to think of a person in your life who is reasonably important to you. It could be your partner or spouse, your child, your parent, boss or co-worker.

'Now find a way to sit that is alert and relaxed. Just put aside whatever you were mentally holding on to. Allow your thoughts to just stop for a moment. Just tell yourself that everything else can wait for the next ten-odd minutes. Take a few deep breaths and give yourself permission to relax. There's nowhere else to be right now, nothing else to do. Just allow the mind to settle. Inhale and exhale deeply, giving the body permission to relax.

'Recall the person that you thought of before we started the exercise. Picture them in your mind as if they were in front of you right now. Imagine what they look like, what they sound like. Holding this person's image in your mind, recognize that this person is a fellow human being. Repeat the following silently in your mind:

This person is a human being like me.

Like me, this person has a mind and a body.

This person has thoughts, emotions and feelings, just like me.

Like me, this person has been sad, disappointed, angry, hurt or confused at some point in their life.

Like me, this person has also experienced physical, mental and emotional pain and suffering in their life.

They really wish to be free from all that pain and suffering. So do I.

Like me, this person has also experienced many times of happiness and joy.

Like me, they also wish to be happy, healthy, loved and have wonderful relationships.

This person also wishes to be happy, just like me.

'You are both human and similar. Now, let's allow some wishes to come up for this person. You can say, "I wish for this person to have the courage, the strength and the skills to navigate the difficult times in life." If you wish, just gently place your palms on your heart centre—"I deeply wish for this person to be free from pain and suffering. I deeply wish for this person to be happy because they are another human being, just like me." Imagine this person as clearly as you can in your mind.

'Now, think of all those you love—your family, your close friends. Extend good wishes to them. "May they all be happy! May they all be free from suffering! May they all be at peace!"

'There is so much pain and suffering in the world today. So, let us now extend these wishes even further to other friends, other co-workers—"May they be happy! May they be free from suffering! May they be at peace!" Now, let us extend these wishes even further to everyone, all over the world, irrespective of colour, race, religion, gender or age—"May everyone in this world be happy! May everyone in this world be free from suffering! May everyone, everywhere be at peace!" Just keep silently wishing with as much passion as possible.

'And finally, don't forget yourself. "May I be happy! May I be free from suffering! May I be at peace!" Just allow the energy of your mindfulness and good wishes to fill your entire being, thinking of the person you thought of at the beginning, thinking of everybody else, and extending these wishes to everybody. Now, take your attention to your breath. Notice those inhalations and exhalations. Notice the beginning of the inhalation, how it goes in, how it ends, how the exhalation begins, how it goes out, how it ends. Notice there is a space between the inhalation and the exhalation, and vice versa.

'Take your awareness to your body. Notice that there is a body, simply here, sitting. Notice how you are feeling now. Is there a sense of lightness, perhaps? Is there a sense of joy? Is there a sense of gratitude? Is there a sense of generosity? Making a gentle movement with your fingers or your toes, notice the sensations that arise. Breathe in and out deeply one more time.

'Whenever you are ready, slowly open your eyes. Let the outside world slowly connect with the inside world. There's no hurry right now to go anywhere else or be anywhere else. Simply enjoy the present moment, allowing the feeling to stay, experiencing the moment of empathy.'

As Sid slowly opened his moist eyes, he glanced at Krish, who remained still, radiating a calm presence, and then looked out at the trees swaying gently in the breeze. For a few moments, Sid stayed silent, letting the echoes of the practice settle within him.

Sid had chosen to focus on one of his friends, Priya, during the exercise. She had always been his cheerleader, but recently, her life had taken a challenging turn. A difficult job transition and then being diagnosed with cancer had left her feeling rather defeated. As he thought of her, he felt a deep wave of connection arise, realizing how much she was probably trying to stay strong despite her struggles.

Through the exercise, Sid not only felt her pain more vividly but also experienced an overwhelming sense of compassion and warmth. The wishes he sent her—for strength, courage and happiness—felt as though they extended beyond words, flowing from a place deep within his heart.

When the practice expanded to others—friends, colleagues, strangers and eventually, the whole world—Sid was surprised at how natural it felt. For a moment, the divisions that often felt so real—differences in opinion, race, background—seemed inconsequential. He noticed a profound sense of unity and peace that left him teary-eyed.

And when it came time to wish happiness and peace upon himself, he hesitated briefly but eventually embraced the act with surprising ease.

As he sat there, basking in the after-effects of the practice, Sid noticed how his heart felt lighter, his breathing calmer, and his thoughts less cluttered. It was as though he had taken a mental and emotional shower, washing away layers of stress and judgment.

Breaking the silence, Sid said softly, 'I thought of my close friend, Priya. She's been going through a very tough time lately, and for the first time, I wasn't caught up in trying to "fix" things for her. I just wanted her to feel seen, supported, and loved. And then, when it extended to everyone else . . . I don't know, Krish. It was like the walls between me and the world fell away.'

Krish smiled gently. 'That's the power of empathy and connection, Sid.'

> **When you let go of trying to solve everything and simply be with the other person's emotions, it transforms how you connect—with them and with yourself.**

Sid nodded, still processing the experience. 'I feel . . . lighter. Like I don't have to carry so much. And it's humbling, you know? Knowing that everyone is just trying to navigate their own storms.'

Krish leaned forward, his voice calm yet filled with conviction.

'Imagine if you felt like this more often. You don't have to go on a bike trip or a holiday to feel a certain way. It is completely possible to be more aware of the present even in everyday life. When you are angry about something that happened, you are angry about the past. When you are worrying about the future, it's about the future. When you were compassionate and kind, it was in the present. The present moment is all there is. There is no past, there is no future. It is just a series of present moments.

'In this moment, if you can be kind, compassionate and generous, you get to shape your life. At one level, mindfulness is nothing but how you live your life. Moment to moment to moment. Generosity and gratitude are wonderful things, both for the giver as well as the receiver. It's a secret that not many people know or understand. The kinder or the more compassionate you are—the more generous you are—the better you feel. There's a saying commonly attributed to the famous civil rights worker Maya Angelou that really moves me.

> **'People will forget what you said, people will forget what you did, but people will never forget how you made them feel.'**

'And I can tell you from my own experience that this is extremely true. People forget all kinds of things but they never forget how you made them feel. I have had the privilege of working with incredibly smart people, and I've tested this theory.

'This is something you can demonstrate every moment of your life. At one point, I used to travel a lot, and I spent a lot of my time in airports. One of the things I noticed is how janitors have so much work to do. They have to mop the floor when it gets wet, flush toilets when people have not flushed them properly and keep wiping the surface of the counter. They ensure that the entire restroom is clean and smells good. It's quite a thankless job. How many people even look at them? We all use those facilities. Many times, we are on the phone. Nobody notices these people. Now, they are not invisible. They are very much there. One of our more important moments is being taken care of by this person. Yet, we treat them like they are invisible.

'Here is a great opportunity to practise something. Just a look or a nod. You might be speaking on the phone but mouthing "thank you" goes a huge way not just to make the janitor feel good but to build your own capabilities, your own qualities and your own character. Because when you are doing this, you are actually doing something for yourself. The same thing I would like to extend to people who work in our workspaces, factories, offices, our gardeners and security staff. We tend to not notice them because we believe we are doing all the important stuff.

'They're not invisible. They are people. They're doing things that help us continue what we are doing. When you go to a restaurant or cafe, you can acknowledge the presence of the people who are serving you. Often, we place orders without a recognition of who that person is, how they might be doing in this job or how easy or difficult it might be for them.

'Even just looking them in the eye and saying, "Thank you!" is enough. I always make it a point to ask them their name followed by, if I have the time, a quick question, "Where are you from?" or "How long have you been working here?" And immediately, there's special service and more attention because people never forget how you made them feel, right? It's not just about the tip at the end of the day. It's also about the human touch. Children, people with disabilities, poor people—how do we make them feel? When we see a poor person on the road, what do we do? We avoid looking at them. We look somewhere else or we put our head down. We pretend we haven't seen them. Or we cross the road. Why? Because it disturbs us. It bothers us. However, it's actually an opportunity to expand ourselves.

'The same thing with seniors. Many times, we treat them as if they are stupid. Being old just makes them a little slow, maybe a little hard of hearing or a little confused perhaps. You might be faster and sharper, but is that not an opportunity to be more empathetic? So, how can we stop treating people as if they are invisible? How can we stop treating people as if they are worthless? And how can we stop treating people as if they are stupid? These are just some perspectives that I would like to offer for you to reflect on as you build your empathy.'

Sid nodded slowly, his mind swirling with reflections.

Every interaction, no matter how small, is an opportunity to practise empathy and strengthen that connection to others—and to yourself.

Sid sat considering the depth of the insight. 'It's not just about making others feel seen, but also about shaping our own character and mindset in the process. It's interesting how much we can gain by simply being present and kind.'

Krish leaned forward again, his tone steady yet encouraging. 'And that's the essence of empathy—it's not limited to structured practices or occasional acts of kindness. Every moment, every interaction, is an opportunity to build it. Now, let's look at something else.

'Do not confuse empathy with being permissive or soft. The fear often is that if one is empathetic, one will be taken advantage of. That is quite far from the truth. Empathy does not mean you have to agree with the other person. Empathy just means being there to understand how that person is feeling and then doing what is right for that person. I told you about my friend and how he did not get a promotion. At that moment, it was not about me saying or doing anything. It was just about being present for him. Later, it was about contributing a perspective to bring about a change in behaviour.

'We don't have to really look hard to find opportunities to practise empathy. Every interaction, every moment gives an opportunity to practise it. When somebody speaks to you, do you also listen for feelings? I might be telling you right now, "Oh, you know what, everything is fine. Life is great", and all of that, but if you listen to me and with empathy, you might understand that I'm scared about something and I'm saying all this just to sound brave. So, empathetic listening is the ability to look beyond what is being said and understand what is being felt.

'At the end of the day, when you understand how somebody else is feeling, you engage with them at a deeper level. And you will also realize like me that people will forget what you said, people will forget what you did, but people will never, ever forget how you made them feel.'

Sid asked, 'How can a manager work on bringing the team closer and create an informal environment? How can empathy be used there?'

'Simple,' said Krish. 'What if we were to stop for a moment to check in with everyone and see how they are doing? Maybe it would take a minute for each person, or a few seconds for each person, but just to help them understand that yes, we are all in this together can be a starting point. Just being there to listen and hold the space for somebody to express is important.'

Sid closed his eyes, absorbing Krish's insights. The sun dipped lower in the sky, casting a soft, amber glow over the lotus pond. Krish and Sid sat side by side on the weathered wooden bench, their silence companionable. The stillness of the water mirrored the calm between them, broken only by the occasional ripple from a dragonfly landing lightly on a lily pad.

Sid leaned back, his gaze fixed on the green leaves floating serenely on the surface. 'It's funny,' he said quietly, 'how this pond seems so peaceful, yet there's probably a lot going on beneath the surface.'

Krish smiled, his eyes reflecting the fading light. 'A lot like life, isn't it? Stillness on the outside, movement within. The lotus thrives in the mud, yet all we see is its beauty.'

Sid nodded thoughtfully, the metaphor settling deeply. 'And maybe that's where resilience and trust are built—in the unseen, the foundations we don't often acknowledge.'

The breeze stirred gently, rustling the leaves overhead. Krish glanced at Sid as he stood, his voice warm and steady. 'You've had a lot to absorb today, Sid. Take some time tonight to sit with it all. The lotus pond and I will still be here tomorrow.'

Sid smiled, the corners of his mouth lifting with gratitude. 'I think I'll do just that. Thanks, Krish—for everything.'

Sid watched Krish walk away, his words lingering in the quiet stillness of the evening. Reaching for the water bottle he had carried, Sid lifted it to his lips. The coolness of the bottle against his fingertips brought his awareness back to the present moment. Pausing, he recalled the practice of mindful drinking Krish had spoken about.

He closed his eyes briefly, taking a slow sip. The water was cool and refreshing, spreading a calm sensation as it travelled down his throat. Sid noticed the subtle taste, the weight of the bottle and the rhythmic movement of his hand. A small smile curved his lips—something so simple, yet deeply grounding.

Sid sat a while longer after Krish had left, watching as the first stars began to dot the evening sky. Then, as the air cooled and the light dimmed, Sid stood, stretching briefly. With one last look at the pond, he turned towards the path leading to his cottage.

The gravel under his feet crunched softly with each step. The familiar scents of the fresh grass and earth lingered as the stillness of the night grew. The morning's encounter with the little boy and the lame puppy had left a deep imprint on Sid. The day had turned out to be profound and insightful as Krish had once again magically weaved wisdom from that incident.

Inside the cottage, he lit a small lamp, its soft glow illuminating the blank pages of his journal. Sitting at the desk, he took a deep breath, letting the events and insights of the day flow onto the page.

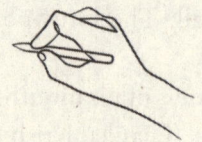

Empathy isn't just an act—it's a way of being, a lens through which we can view and shape the world.

Resilience, trust, empathy—all of it grows from the unseen depths within us.

Empathy is the bridge to connection and trust is its reward. It starts with understanding—ourselves and others—and grows in the spaces where judgment gives way to shared humanity.

Empathy isn't just a skill—it's a way of being. Compassion builds trust and connection. Resilience begins with calm.

My little practice:

Breath 1: Notice my breath.

Breath 2: Become aware of my body.

Breath 3: Think of a person of my choosing.

Breath 4: Remind myself that this person is a fellow human being.

Day 8: Empathy and Building Great Teams

> **Reflection questions:**
>
> What is one thing I can start doing with another at a heart-to-heart level?
>
> Which broken relationship do I want to restore today?

Sid set down his pen and closed the journal softly, letting the final words linger in his mind.

He stretched, feeling a pleasant tiredness settle into his body. The lamp's glow flickered gently, casting warm shadows across the room.

Stepping to the window, Sid looked out at the stillness of the farm. The faint sound of crickets filled the air and a cool breeze brushed against his face. The bamboo tree swayed gently. Tomorrow felt like a new canvas, ready to be painted with the colours of all he was discovering. With a small smile, he turned off the lamp and lay down, letting the day's reflections cradle him into restful sleep.

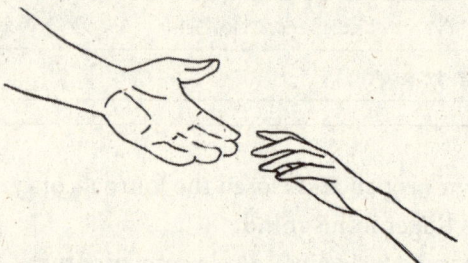

Day 9: Compassionate Leadership

The early morning sunlight spilled softly through the window of Sid's room, bathing it in a golden glow. Sid stirred awake, his mind surprisingly clear and refreshed. He stretched, letting the cool morning breeze drifting in through the window brush against his skin, grounding him in the present moment.

Sitting on the edge of the bed, he closed his eyes and visualized the image of the lotus pond. The memory of the previous day came back—Krish's teachings on empathy, the practice of connection and the gentle wisdom woven into the incident of the boy and the puppy. It all seemed to converge into one powerful realization: there was so much he needed to rethink about his approach to life and leadership.

Day 9: Compassionate Leadership

Sid pulled out his journal, flipping through the pages filled with reflections from his time here. His own handwriting seemed to speak to him:

Empathy isn't just a skill; it's a way of being.
Compassion builds trust and connection.
Resilience begins with calm.

He traced the words with his finger, lingering on the thought of compassion.

Sid was seen as a high potential leader in his organization. He had himself set his sights on a CXO role in a few years. He had always prided himself on being efficient and goal-oriented. But he could see now how often he had overlooked the human side of leadership. How many times had he pushed his team too hard, assuming their struggles were obstacles to overcome rather than experiences to understand? How often had he judged performance without looking for the 'why' behind the behaviour?

The scenes from yesterday kept replaying in his mind—the little boy choosing the lame puppy, Krish's insight about balancing empathy and action and the profound connection he had felt during the guided practice. Compassion wasn't just an optional quality for a leader—it was essential. Sid realized that to inspire and uplift the incredibly smart and talented people he worked with, he needed to weave compassion into the very fabric of his leadership.

With that thought, he felt a resolve settle in him. He wanted to explore this deeper—how to lead with compassion without compromising on results. He needed Krish's perspective and the morning felt like the perfect time for such a conversation.

After mindfully brushing his teeth, showering and getting ready for the day, Sid eventually stepped out into the fresh morning air.

Sure enough, Krish was seated on the veranda, a steaming cup in his hand, gazing out at the morning landscape with an expression of quiet contentment. Sid hesitated for a moment, not wanting to disturb the peaceful scene. But Krish turned and saw him, his face lighting up with a warm smile.

'Good morning, Sid! You're up early,' Krish said, gesturing to the empty chair beside him. 'Come, join me. How are you feeling today?'

Sid took the seat, the chair creaking slightly under his weight. 'Good morning, Krish,' he began, his tone thoughtful. 'I've been reflecting on everything we talked about yesterday—empathy, trust and how it all ties into leadership. I realize there's so much I've been missing in how I approach my team. I want to learn how to bring more compassion into my leadership. Can we talk about that today?'

Krish nodded, his expression encouraging. 'Ah, compassionate leadership. A topic close to my heart.' And with that, the morning unfolded into another profound conversation, the golden sunlight their silent witness.

'Compassion is often thought of as something reserved for certain people. We have been taught to think or believe that compassion makes you soft or that compassion is not such a good thing. However, it is an integral part of every human being.

'Compassion, like empathy, is a word that is often used very liberally, but do we actually understand it? You know, it comes from the two words "com" and "passion": "com" means together and passion is suffer, pain. Compassion basically means "suffering together". But today, as always, we're going to take a slightly different journey; we're not going to get stuck with traditional old definitions,' Krish explained.

'The whole idea is to use mindfulness to expand our perspective and become wiser. So, I'm going to encourage another perspective of compassion—empathy plus action. What do I mean by that? Empathy is understanding what the other person feels, even when you do not necessarily agree with them. Now, if you act on that, it becomes compassion.'

Empathy is the foundation for compassion.
Compassion is the aspect of doing something after
you have felt empathy.

'I just want you to silently answer these two questions for yourself. Be completely honest. It's a great opportunity to understand yourself better and build some amazing skills.

'One: When you meet somebody who's in difficulty, how do you feel? Don't go for diplomatic, polite answers because no one is going to hear them. You are talking to yourself. Be completely honest. Do you immediately feel like helping them? Do you immediately feel like, oh, what will happen to me if I help them? Do you feel like looking the other way? Be brutally honest.

'Two: What are some ways in which you react? Let me give you an example. Let's say a person in difficulty approaches you. Picture the situation. What do you feel? Avoidance, annoyance? Do you want to avoid that person? Or do you suddenly get engrossed in your phone? Reflecting on yourself, when you meet somebody who is in a difficult situation, how do you react?'

Sid sat quietly, letting Krish's words sink in. The morning breeze brushed past him, carrying the faint scent of jasmine as he gazed out in the direction of the serene lotus pond. Krish's question echoed in his mind: *When you meet somebody who's in difficulty, how do you feel?*

He closed his eyes, recalling moments from his own life—walking past a homeless person on the street, hearing a colleague open up about personal struggles or even witnessing his friends navigate their challenges. How often had he truly stopped to engage with their pain, without avoidance, judgment or feeling overwhelmed?

Sid felt a pang of discomfort as he acknowledged the truth. In many instances, he had avoided such situations entirely. When faced with someone's pain, his immediate reaction was often to shield himself, to not get involved. And when he did engage, there were times when the weight of their emotions felt like too much to bear, leaving him drained and helpless.

He opened his eyes and looked at Krish, his voice quiet but resolute. 'I think I've been avoiding this question my entire life, Krish. When I see someone in difficulty, my first instinct is often to protect myself— and when I respond, it's either by ignoring it or by stepping in too much, to the point where I feel overwhelmed. It's like I don't know how to find the balance.'

Day 9: Compassionate Leadership

Krish nodded, his gaze calm and steady. 'That's a very honest reflection, Sid. And it's the first step towards understanding the role of compassion. What you're describing is something many people experience. Let's explore this further.

'Empathy translates in two ways. When you see another person in difficulty, you can start to understand how they feel and why they feel that way. Then you too could start feeling like them, because you're so connected with them. This is empathic distress.

'Imagine somebody has fallen into a hole. Can you help them by also falling into the hole? Not really! You can help them by understanding that they are in a hole. But you might want to be outside the hole and drop a rope in so that you can help them climb out.

'So, it's important to understand the difference between empathy and empathic distress. Suicide rates are the highest in some professions—nurses, veterinarians and caregivers. This is because of empathic distress. They spend so much time with people who are in pain and suffering that if they are not able to clearly distinguish that they are not the one suffering, they start owning that pain. You then don't act in a good way towards even the person who was suffering in the first place. And what does it result in? It results in poor health and burnout.

'What is the alternative to this? Empathy can also be experienced positively and that is what is called compassion. Compassion is where you say, "Hmm, I understand what this person is going through, I feel for them, even though I may or may not agree. And it's all about that person." Then you start to go out of your way to help or do what is right for that person. And you know what? That actually produces good health in you!

'It's so interesting that the same foundation can either result in something not so good or very good. Compassion leads to positive hormones being released in the body. There is a sense of contribution and a feel-good factor instead of stress and burnout in empathic distress.

'I think of compassion as having three parts. The first, of course, is empathy—feeling and understanding that the other person is in difficulty. The second part is action. Just sitting back, in your chair and saying "hmm" could be empathy, but that is not compassion. When you get off your chair and do something for the person who's suffering, then it becomes compassion.

'And then we go one step further. The constant practise of this is what helps you build it into a habit and internalize it. So, let's say, one evening, you are in your office. After you finish work, you shut down your laptop, put away your mobile and prepare to relax for some time. Let's say you're just going to do some mindfulness practice.

'Just as you're starting to settle into the practice, a friend calls, saying that they are stuck on the highway and their car won't start. They are maybe two hours away from where you are. You understand that they are in trouble, that they might be panicking because it is hard to find a mechanic at that time.

'If you decide to go and help, you're in a sense saying, "I'll find some other way of doing my mindfulness practice, but I'm going to go out there and help them." That is action. So, putting yourself aside and doing something to help is the action portion of compassion. If you do this regularly, it becomes a habit. And then the energy of compassion starts to flow in your body. And this is a very interesting thing, because personally, I have gone through this journey of training myself to think in a certain way. And I know the energy shift that it has brought about. I remember a time when I used to run teams of a few hundred people and there would be a lot of stress and pressure. I felt I was caught up in that hole and could not move into action.

'By making it a practice to ask myself, "How can I help this person", I was able to make a significant transformation for myself as well as in my career. So, ask yourself. How do I deal compassionately with my partner, my family, my parents? And importantly, how do I deal compassionately with other people at work? How do I deal compassionately with my peers? How do I deal compassionately with my subordinates? How do I deal compassionately with the bosses, with leadership?'

Sid listened intently, Krish's words resonating deeply as he connected them to his own experiences. He leaned forward, his fingers tracing the grain of the wood absent-mindedly.

'So, it's not just about feeling for someone but taking thoughtful action. It's about creating that balance where you're not overwhelmed by their pain but motivated to help in a way that truly matters,' Sid joined the dots. He let the thought settle, feeling a growing sense of curiosity about how this could influence his own journey. He looked at Krish, ready for the next insight.

'In my own leadership journey, it allowed me to move from leading a few hundred people to a much more senior leadership position. And here too, I found I could lead with compassion.'

> 'Having compassion for others frees us from fearing . . . it turns our attention outward, expanding our perspective, making our own problems . . . part of something bigger than us that we are all in together.'—Thupten Jinpa

Krish continued, 'It's such a wonderful perspective shift when we start to look at it this way. When we stop thinking just about ourselves in a very narrow way, this starts to create inspiring leadership.'

The gentle movement of the leaves mirrored the thoughts settling in Sid's mind. 'Compassion has a way of broadening our horizons, Sid,' Krish said, his voice steady yet reflective. 'When we lead with compassion, it's not just about the impact on others—it's transformative for us too. It shapes how we see the world.'

> **Mindfulness and compassion are connected—like two sides of the same coin.**
> **When you're fully present and focused, clarity arises.**
> **And with that clarity, compassion naturally follows.**
> **It's not forced; it just happens.**

Sid paused, a small smile forming. 'It's about truly seeing the moment and the people in it. When you do that, compassion becomes a natural extension of mindfulness.'

Krish nodded, pleased. 'Mindfulness and compassion. When you practise one, the other automatically seems to follow. Being completely involved in what you're doing—it might be a game of chess, writing an email, listening to somebody, making a presentation or anything else. Automatically, the energy of mindfulness rises and compassion follows.'

> **'Wisdom without compassion is ruthlessness and compassion without wisdom is folly.'—Fred Kofman**

'Blindly rushing into compassion or just blindly rushing into action can be detrimental. When you stop to think, use mindfulness and awareness and add it to compassion, you take better action.

'A few weeks ago, a friend of mine who is very fond of dogs and has two of his own called me up. He had found an injured dog on the street. He carried the dog two kilometres to the vet in the rain and got the dog treated. But then, he didn't know where to keep the dog, as his own pets would not have let him bring another dog home.

'He was forced to leave the dog outside his house on the street. The dog ended up tearing its bandage open in a few minutes and had to be taken to the vet again. Now, while I really admired his intention, this is an example of how compassion when it's not fully thought through can fall short of achieving the best possible outcome or the desired outcome.

'The intention was very good. My friend spent his own money, carried the dog in the rain and felt good about it too. But where did the result end up? It didn't solve the dog's problem, right? And in the long run, it didn't match my friend's intention either.'

'I understand. So, that is what you mean by compassion without wisdom. What would have been wiser for him to do? Probably asking around and finding a shelter where the dog could recover in peace. That could have been an act of compassion plus wisdom,' Sid said hesitantly.

Krish paused, letting Sid's words settle in the stillness between them. He watched him thoughtfully, giving him space to process the nuanced implications. The gentle rustle of leaves filled the air, punctuating the quiet moment with a natural rhythm.

After a few moments, Krish continued, his voice steady and reflective. 'Now, let's look at the other side of the equation—what happens when wisdom operates without compassion.

'Consider Alexander the Great. He was known for not having much compassion in his initial years. He was known for being aggressive and action-oriented. And that is, to some extent, what allowed him to also conquer most parts of the then-known world. That's what made him Alexander the Great. But eventually, the same man asked to be taken around the city after his death with his empty hands hanging from his body as he wanted everyone to see that he had left the world with nothing. Wisdom had prevailed, albeit a bit late!

'When wisdom operates without the ingredients of kindness, caring and love for the other person, then it can be ruthless. You can ruthlessly wipe out the competition or you can ruthlessly destroy your opponent. You can think of many leaders who have great insights and wisdom, but compassion is missing.

'Whether you go into Zen philosophy or Buddhist philosophy, yogic traditions or chakras, they all point to compassion. In modern leadership too, it's about leading with the gut, heart and the mind. Gut being instinct and intuition, heart being compassion and kindness, and mind being insights, vision and the ability to foresee things. So, when all of these get combined, it makes for a really powerful and holistic way of leading, whether you're leading other people, leading yourself or just leading a life.'

When Krish paused, Sid contemplated the complexity of what he had just said to him. 'But sometimes, what a person asks for and what they truly need can be really different. How do we help them differentiate that and give what is really needed?'

'Often, the person who is suffering is in a certain state of mind because of their difficulty. They may or may not be practitioners of mindfulness like you and, therefore, their state of mind may be a little disturbed. In that state of mind, they may not always know what is best or right for them.

'On the other hand, being on the outside, and as a practitioner of mindfulness and compassion, you will probably be able to see it from a much wiser perspective. And here is where all the skills that we have been talking about start to add up, whether it is our awareness, our management of our own emotions, our resilience or our empathy. How do you get the person to see the right perspective? How are you able to explain to them? Are you able to help them understand?

'As you attempt to navigate this, things will shift. The other person may start to see your point of view, or they may not. And if they don't, what else do you want to do?

Even your own point of view may change a little bit if you remain completely open and aware. So then together, you navigate the situation. And even within that, there can be a number of ways in which you may choose to deal with the moment. Sometimes, you give a child a toffee to stop them from crying, although that's not very healthy for them. But then later, you decide to solve the problem in a different way. Even with adults it might not be very different. So, that is where all your capabilities as a leader come in. A leader is not only so by title or designation, right? In that situation, you assume leadership. You are going to lead that person out of their difficult situation. I'm afraid there isn't a standard formula, but I'm hoping that everything that you have been learning now can show up at that moment for you.'

Krish's words hung in the air, their weight settling in Sid's mind. He took a deep breath, his thoughts beginning to align with the ideas shared.

We often think of leadership as managing people. But people don't want to be managed. They want to be inspired. They want to be led. And understanding them and knowing how to serve them is at the heart of compassionate leadership.

Sid leaned back, absorbing Krish's insights. 'But Krish, what happens when the person you're dealing with is hurting you or is clearly in the wrong? How do you keep showing compassion in the face of negative behaviour? How do you manage to tolerate that and not let it break your resolve?'

'Did I at any point say that compassion is about tolerating? I did not. Compassion is about doing the right thing for that person. Actually, if you are not telling that person that they're hurting you, and that they're doing injustice to you, you're doing the wrong thing. Compassion is telling them how you feel. Compassion is not keeping quiet. Compassion is not being submissive. By not telling them, you are missing an opportunity to coach them or mentor them to open their eyes and give them perspective.

'Then we come to the question of how do we tell them? Obviously, that needs to be done skilfully. And that is, again, where mindfulness and your ability to have meaningful conversations comes in. How aware are you of yourself?

'So, understand this: When somebody treats you badly, be it a boss or a colleague or someone at home, compassion may or may not be about tolerating that. If in that moment, tolerating is the right thing to do, because any sort of response that you give might escalate the situation, then compassion at that point might mean walking away and choosing not to fight. In another instance, compassion may actually involve standing your ground and saying, "Hey, I don't think this is how it should be", and having a conversation to bring about a realization that what they are doing is not right. That is compassion in another sense.

Krish's words settled over Sid like a quiet revelation. He took a moment, his gaze steady, as the depth of the message began to resonate within him.

He then nodded, once again reflecting on Krish's explanation. 'So, compassion isn't about tolerating or staying silent—it's about doing what's right for the other person and for the situation. Sometimes that means skilfully speaking up and expressing how their behaviour affects you. Other times, it might mean stepping away to avoid escalation. It's not about being aggressive or submissive or accepting mistreatment but using awareness and mindfulness to decide the best course of action at that moment.'

Krish smiled and nodded gently. 'Absolutely. I will let you process and refine your reflections further now while I go and attend to a few chores.'

Sid strolled along the quiet path, the late afternoon sun casting a golden glow over the trees. He remembered an incident from a few years ago.

He was working in a fast-paced tech company and a young software engineer named Maya in his team had been repeatedly struggling to meet critical deadlines. Their manager hadn't pushed her harder, much to Sid's annoyance at that time. Instead, the manager had taken the time to speak with her, offered flexible work hours and even coordinated with the team to redistribute some workload. Sid had not agreed with the approach. Soon though, Maya, feeling deeply supported, had been able to deliver exceptional work while managing her personal crisis. This act of compassion had not only saved the project but also fostered a stronger bond between Maya and the team, leading to increased productivity and a more positive work culture. Looking back, Sid saw how the leader's genuine empathy and compassion had been a powerful driver of success.

Day 9: Compassionate Leadership

By the time the sun dipped below the horizon, Sid returned to the veranda, his heart lighter and his perspective clearer. The walk and reflection had deepened his understanding of compassion as an act that, while simple, held the power to transform both the giver and the receiver.

As the day slowly drew to a close, the sky turned into a melange of colours with the orange of the day making way for the purple of the night. The crickets added their hum of approval. The air too had begun to get cooler. The daytime conversations were reaching deeper into Sid's mind like roots spreading out in fertile soil. He could feel the effects of the insights he had experienced today—a sense of clarity, purpose and renewed curiosity.

The soft glow of the lantern on the veranda of the cottage welcomed him. Sid went straight to the small wooden table in his room and poured himself a glass of water. Sipping it with awareness was thoroughly refreshing. After a moment of enjoying the stillness it created, he reached for his journal.

I want to explore how I can start applying this balance of compassion and wisdom in my own leadership. I need to think about my team—what they need, how they feel and how I can lead them with greater awareness.

For now, I'll sit with this thought: Compassion, practised mindfully, transforms both the giver and the receiver. I'm beginning to feel that shift within myself.

The familiar scratch of pen on paper was comforting as Sid began to write, pouring out his reflections from the day. The bamboo leaves rustled gently in the breeze.

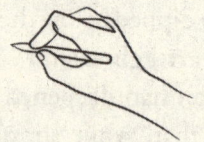

Compassion isn't about tolerating someone's wrong behaviour or staying silent. It's about doing what is right for them and the situation, even if that means speaking up or walking away. It's empathy in action, balanced by wisdom.

Mindfulness—being fully present—creates space for compassion to flow.

Compassion without wisdom is folly. It is useless. Wisdom without compassion is ruthlessness. It is destructive.

Leadership is fluid and responsive to any given situation. It's about adapting with humility, care and clarity.

Compassion, practised mindfully, transforms both the giver and the receiver. I'm beginning to feel that shift within myself.

> **My little practice:**
> Breathing in, I feel connected to the person.
> Breathing out, I ask myself what would serve them the best.
>
> **Reflection question:** Am I more interested in being loved or in giving love?

Sid closed his journal, his heart feeling a little lighter yet more grounded. Outside, the night had fully arrived, its stillness wrapping around the cottage like a warm blanket. As Sid lay down, his thoughts settled into a calm silence and the echoes of the day's lessons gently accompanied him into sleep.

Day 10: Purpose and Transformation

The morning sky was painted with hues of gold and soft lavender as Sid stepped out of the cottage. The crisp air carried the faint aroma of wet earth and blooming flowers, grounding him in the present yet tinged with possibilities. A gentle breeze rustled the leaves in the trees, as though whispering a secret to him, while the distant sound of bells wafted across, merging with the call of birds waking to a new day.

Sid took a deep breath, letting the cool air fill his lungs, and for the first time in years, it felt as though he was truly breathing—fully alive, fully present. Over the last nine days, he had been stretched, challenged and renewed. Each conversation with Krish, each practice of mindfulness and

Day 10: Purpose and Transformation

every quiet reflection by the lotus pond had planted seeds deep within him. Today, he felt like those seeds were beginning to sprout, filling him with a profound sense of clarity and a hum of energy that he hadn't experienced before.

As he walked, memories came flooding back of his time with Krish—awareness of the thoughts and feelings he'd resisted, of the difficult reflections he had faced about his own habits and shortcomings and of the breakthroughs that followed, the golden light of compassion, the realization that leadership was not about power but connection. The dots connected almost magically to trace his journey from discovering himself to learning how to master himself and finally touching the lives of others.

Sid thought of the lotus pond. He remembered its still waters reflecting the sky. Any odd unseen movement would occasionally create ripples that spread outward. *Just like the lessons I've learned,* he thought.

Small actions, mindful intentions—each one creating a ripple that could reach far beyond me.

There was no mistaking it: this was not the same Sid who had arrived here nine days ago. The man who had felt restless, was burned out and unsure of his path now stood at the cusp of something greater. The pieces of his transformation were beginning to come together, forming a tapestry of purpose. But a quiet urgency stirred within him—a realization that learning without action was incomplete. *What good are all these insights if they're not put to the test of action?* he thought.

The morning sunlight kissed the earth with warmth, as if nudging him forward. *This is it,* he told himself. *I can't just go back to life as it was. I must apply what I've learned.*

The very thought sent a surge of energy through him. Sid straightened his back and stretched his arms upwards, looking at the sky. Closing his eyes for a minute, he let the energy course through him.

Eventually he walked back to the cottage where he found Krish sitting on the veranda. The veranda had become something of a sacred space to Sid, a place where conversations had changed the way he saw himself and the world. Today, it would hold one more.

Krish, sitting cross-legged with his cup of tea, glanced up as Sid approached. His calm, knowing smile seemed to acknowledge the shift he sensed in Sid.

'Good morning, Sid,' Krish said, his voice warm and welcoming. 'How are you feeling today?'

Sid smiled back, his steps deliberate as he took his usual seat. 'Morning, Krish,' he said, his voice steady and filled with resolve. 'Something is happening. Everything I've experienced over these last nine days—it's starting to come together. I feel like I'm standing at the edge of something important. I have to take this transformation into my life and into action. There's no other way forward.'

Krish nodded approvingly, setting his cup down. 'That's a powerful place to be, Sid,' he said thoughtfully. 'The energy you're feeling right now—this sense of purpose—can be the fuel that drives you.'

'This thing about "purpose" is something I wanted to discuss with you. When I hear people talk about it, it sounds like something hard which only a lucky few manage to find. I have also heard about concepts like *ikigai* and living a life of purpose. I'd love to know what you think.'

'Haha, sure! Let me share my own experience with purpose first, and then we'll explore it a little more and bring the angle of mindfulness into it.' He paused for a minute, closing his eyes and gathering his thoughts.

'I didn't really discover my purpose for a long time,' Krish eventually began.

'Eventually, after years of mindfulness practices, I slowly started looking at what my interests, strengths and values were. I started building out a sort of mental map of where I had been in life, what all I had done and what I really wanted to do.

'I started making those connections for myself and as I did that, slowly something happened. I started to get a better sense of what my purpose was. I am telling you this story because it is very rare that people discover their purpose in a dream or on one fine morning when they wake up. It makes for a really good story but in reality, that's not exactly how it works.

'Once you start to even get a sense of your purpose, it is a beautiful experience altogether. In discovering my purpose, I realized that there were so many things that I had to let go of. I was holding on to so many beliefs and notions of who I was, who I wanted to be, how the world sees things and what society will think. I had to let go of it all for my purpose to reveal itself. There is an integral beauty not only in discovering your purpose but also in going through that process of discovery. This is a good time to tell you a story.'

There once was a caterpillar who got tired of being a caterpillar. He thought he was ugly and useless. So, he asked around: 'There has to be some other purpose to my existence and I wonder how I can discover it. How can I transform?' Somebody said, 'There is a very wise owl who lives on the other side of the fence, and he supposedly has all the answers. Why don't you go ask him?'

The caterpillar undertook the long journey. Travelling to the other side of the fence took many hours. Finally, he reached the tree where the owl was sitting with his eyes closed, meditating. The caterpillar couldn't disturb the owl, so he waited. Eventually, the owl opened his eyes and looked at the caterpillar. The caterpillar said, 'Please, wise owl, can you help me. I am tired of being ugly and useless. I want to find my purpose. I want to transform. Can you tell me how?'

The owl looked at him, closed his eyes and went back into meditation. The poor caterpillar sat for a long time. Finally, the owl opened his eyes, looked at the caterpillar and said, 'Get out of the way.' The caterpillar said, 'What?' The owl said, 'Get out of the way.' The caterpillar was very hurt. He thought the owl was asking him to go away.

He hung his head in sadness and left. On the way back, he thought, 'I saw the owl meditating for so long; let me try it.' So he sat and meditated. That's when he realized what the owl was trying to say to him. The owl did not want him to physically get out of the way. What he was saying was that the caterpillar needed to get out of his mind to let the transformation happen.

As the caterpillar understood this, he went deeper and deeper into meditation. A cocoon formed around him. Metamorphosis happened and eventually a beautiful butterfly emerged. The whole process of turning from a caterpillar to a butterfly required him to get out of his own way.

'That is such a beautiful story!' said Sid and grinned, as he looked up at the sky, a playful glimmer in his eyes. 'You know, Krish, I think the caterpillar and I might have more in common than I realized. I've been crawling through life with a head full of questions—and I can't say I've met any owls. But you . . .' He paused, pointing a teasing finger at Krish. 'You might just be the wisest bird I know.'

Krish chuckled softly, shaking his head. 'Flattery will get you nowhere, Sid,' he replied with a mock sternness.

Sid laughed, pushing himself up from the chair with an easy stretch, his hands resting on his hips as he looked towards the horizon. 'You know, Krish, that caterpillar might just be my spirit animal. Here I am, asking all these questions about purpose, and maybe all I need to do is get out of my own way.' He turned back to Krish with a playful grin. 'But hey, if I start building a cocoon, don't leave me hanging!'

Krish smiled knowingly, the lines on his face softening with warmth. 'Ah, Sid, you're already beginning to understand. But what does the story really tell you? It means you have to stop your mind from telling you all the stories of what you can't do, why you should do something and why you have to only do what is expected of you. You have to allow something else to arise, which is mindfulness, deeper consciousness and awareness. And when you do that, you become a rebel. And then transformation is possible.

'I want you to do an exercise later today. Write down: When have you been at your best and what have you been doing when you felt at your best in life? Are you guiding other people, are you playing a sport, or working on numbers? What are the occasions when you have felt your best? Just take some time to reflect on all of this.

'Start thinking about how you felt at that time. What kind of emotions did you have? Did you feel energized, charged up, happy, grateful? Then also look at what you struggle with. What makes you feel not so good? Sometimes we struggle when we have to work with other people. For others, it could be when they have to work alone.

'Discovering your purpose is a messy process. Very rarely is one so lucky that you wake up one day and know exactly why you are on this planet. But it is a process that is beautiful and worth doing in itself. You would have heard so many things said about the importance of having a purpose in this lifetime. In fact, there's a saying:

The purpose of life is to find your purpose.

'This is not about finding the pot of gold at the end of the rainbow but about the journey that you undertake to that point. But why do we not undertake this journey? In life, we often hesitate and avoid putting in effort. We avoid finding our sense of purpose. As soon as the need to find purpose raises its voice, we hush it up. We tell it to keep quiet and we do this for various reasons—parental pressure, social expectations, the traps laid by education, religion and so on. Eventually, the voice dies down completely.

'We do this because we fear: *What will happen if I let go of the known? How will I manage? What will other people think? How will I pay the bills?* These fears hold us back from discovering our purpose. I too was no exception when I made that transition. More than the fear that was in me, it was the fear that others were trying to put in me!

'What mindfulness does is help you recognize that fear. You say, *I am not going to deny the fear or suppress it. I am aware of it and I am going to shine the light of awareness on it.* There could also be the guilt we feel that we might not be able to take care of our responsibilities if we go after our purpose. Some people need to take care of parents or their family and think that prevents them from finding their purpose. Others blame circumstances: *If not for this, I would have been Michelangelo or da Vinci.* It's easy to blame other people and circumstances.

'These are some of the factors that hold us back. But each of us can approach these shackles differently as we become more aware. Purpose is like a gift. You have to slowly unpack it and see what's inside that box. That itself can be extremely liberating and transforming.'

Sid absorbed Krish's words in thoughtful silence, the weight of their meaning settling over him like a warm blanket. He took a deep breath, his gaze drifting to the mango tree at the edge of the garden, its branches swaying gently in the breeze, a familiar and comforting sight.

'That's a lot to unpack, Krish,' Sid said finally, his voice steady but contemplative. 'You're right—there's so much we bury under fear, guilt or expectations and it feels like it builds walls around us. I've been chipping away at those walls bit by bit these last few days.' He paused. 'Do you think we could go sit under the mango tree? I don't know why, but it's become one of my favourite spots here. Something about sitting there feels . . . grounding.'

Krish's eyes crinkled with approval as he nodded. 'A perfect choice, Sid. The tree has witnessed many moments of stillness—it will gladly witness yours.'

With that, the two walked quietly towards the mango tree, its sprawling branches casting dappled shadows on the earth below. Sid settled comfortably against the rough trunk, the scent of earth and ripe fruit filling the air. He closed his eyes for a brief moment, feeling the connection between himself, the ground and the gentle rustle of leaves above.

Krish's broke the stillness. 'Now that we are here, how about exploring a little practice, Sid?' Krish's voice took on the magical quality it seemed to have when he guided these reflections.

'I'd love that!' responded Sid enthusiastically.

As Sid settled his body and started to breathe, he could feel a deep sense of calm coming over him. The gentle sounds around him fell away as his mind slowly slipped into a state of silence.

'First settle your body and mind with a few deep breaths. By now, you have learnt how to do this on your own,' said Krish, giving Sid time to settle.

'Imagine now that you are in a forest—beautiful trees, cool air,' he resumed after some time.

'You can hear the birds. Notice the forest floor and a small path that goes into the trees. Out of curiosity, you start to follow this path. With every step, you feel lighter. The body is more relaxed and the mind is calmer. You hear the birds sing and you can hear a stream in the distance somewhere. As you go deeper, you come to a clearing in the forest,' Krish paused for Sid to visualize the scene.

'There is a hut in front of you,' he soon resumed. 'As you observe the structure, you notice a small door. Once you go near the door, you get a sense that there is something inside. A warm presence that's inviting. It's calling out to you. As you step into the structure, you see you are in a hall. It is completely covered with mirrors on the inside. You see your reflection in every direction. The mirrors are of all kinds—some are square, some are rectangle, some are framed while others are not.

'You just stand there for a minute looking at all these reflections. There is one particular mirror that catches your attention and you move towards it. As you near the mirror, you are able to see more details. You notice its shape and its frame. As you stand in front of it, you notice that the mirror is a little cloudy but it slowly starts becoming clearer.'

Sid's mind was visualizing the imagery that Krish was describing.

'Then you see an image in the mirror. What is this image? It is an image of yourself. What are you doing? What kind of a situation are you in? How are you feeling in the image? You observe it like a movie. Who are the other people in the image? What are they saying or doing? Is it the same as what you are doing now in life or is it something different? Without any expectations or judgement, just start accepting and working with whatever you see in the mirror. Stay in front of this mirror, noticing what thoughts arise for you now.'

As Sid stood in front of the mirror, his breath steady and calm, the cloudy surface began to clear, like mist lifting to reveal a quiet landscape. Slowly, an image formed in the mirror, growing sharper with every passing moment. At first, Sid couldn't quite make out the scene—it was bathed in soft light, almost dreamlike. But as he looked closer, he began to see himself, not as he was now, but as a version of himself that felt . . . whole, grounded and alive.

He was standing in a large, airy space—maybe a large room or an auditorium. The room was buzzing with energy and people were gathered around him, listening intently. Sid saw his reflection speaking—not from a place of authority, but with deep connection and presence. His words carried warmth, understanding and purpose. The people in the room—colleagues, friends, even strangers—seemed inspired, their faces lighting up with clarity and hope. Sid wasn't just talking *to* them—he was talking *with* them, listening, guiding and creating a shared experience.

He watched his reflection for a moment, taking in the subtle details. His posture was open, his shoulders relaxed and his face was calm yet radiant. There was a strength in the way he held himself, a confidence that wasn't loud or forced but deeply rooted. He was *leading*, yes—but it wasn't the same old leadership he had always practised. This was different. He was lifting others up, holding space for them to grow and shine.

The image shifted slightly, and Sid noticed a different scene—this time, he was sitting one-on-one with someone. A colleague perhaps, who looked frustrated and lost. Sid could see himself listening—deeply listening—with quiet, compassionate attention. His reflection's presence was like an anchor, steadying the other person as they opened up. Eventually, Sid saw the person's face soften, a smile breaking through as though a burden had been lifted.

The realization hit Sid gently but firmly: he was at his best when he was *present*. When he dropped his need to prove something or to control the outcome—when he led, not through pressure or performance, but through genuine care and understanding.

'Slowly now, in your mind, turn around towards the door, stepping out of the structure.' Krish's voice brought Sid back to the exercise. 'Turn around and take a look at it, knowing that this is a place in your mind that you can come to whenever you need to discover your purpose. With a sense of gratitude and lightness, you turn back onto the path and start walking away from the structure. With every step you take, you feel light and happy. Perhaps something amazing has been revealed to you. Perhaps nothing amazing has been revealed to you. But, you've taken one tiny step on the path of discovering your purpose.

'As you walk slowly, come out of the forest. Now you can see the sunlight and the sky. Take a deep breath as you come back from the journey in the mind. One more time, take a deep breath. Breathe normally, making a gentle movement with your fingers and toes. Gently and softly, open your eyes and allow yourself to come back to being here. Just take a few seconds to fully settle and come back to this moment,' Krish concluded.

Sid sat quietly for a moment, his eyes soft and a bit moist, as though a part of him was lingering in the forest of his mind. The air around him felt charged with a stillness that mirrored the calm within. He drew in a slow breath, looking up at Krish with a sense of wonder and quiet clarity.

'That was . . . something else,' Sid began, his voice reflective, almost hushed. 'When I stepped into that hut and saw all those mirrors, it felt like I was looking at parts of myself I'd been ignoring for a long time. The reflections were overwhelming at first. There was so much of me in there—versions I didn't even know existed. But then, when I saw that one mirror . . .' He paused, searching for the right words. 'It was like the image in it was waiting for me. It wasn't perfect or crystal clear, but it felt real, Krish. I saw myself, not as I am today, but as someone I've always wanted to be—calm, purposeful and truly present.'

Sid clasped his hands together, his gaze drifting to the ground as he quietly gathered his thoughts. After a moment, he looked up, his expression clear and resolved. 'The scene I saw—it wasn't grand or flashy. I wasn't on some massive stage or leading some big revolution. I was just . . . there for people. I was leading, yes, but in a way that felt right—like my purpose wasn't about achieving something for myself but about lifting others. Being fully there for them. And somehow, that gave *me* a sense of meaning.'

Sid's expression turned more thoughtful as he looked out towards the open sky. 'But it also made me realize how much I've been getting in my own way. The doubts, the fears, the false narratives I've been feeding myself. I've been holding on to this idea of success and happiness that I have created—what it should look like, what it has to be—when maybe it's something entirely different for me!'

He turned back to Krish, his voice more certain now. 'I don't have all the answers yet. But for the first time, I feel like I've taken a step—just one tiny step—towards asking the right questions, towards understanding what my purpose might be. And that feels . . . liberating.'

Krish smiled, his gaze warm and knowing. 'That's a beautiful reflection, Sid. You see, the stories that we have been telling ourselves for so many years can be very powerful barriers. They are like the layers in an onion that take a little time to peel. As you go deeper into this practice, it will become easier.'

'And as I peel the layers, I might shed plenty of tears!' said Sid, as he became aware of the tears that had just formed in his eyes.

'Maybe. But more importantly, through this practice, we let go of unwanted things in our body and mind. The residual memories, mental images and thoughts that prevent us from being who we might be.'

It is only when you let go of who you are, that you can become who you might be.

'If you keep clinging on to who you are, you are preventing who you might be from happening. One of the things I found very helpful personally as well as professionally is to convert all MY hurt into healing for other people,' Krish continued.

'We all carry hurt from our past. Sometimes we complain about things people have said to us, and other times we just recall memories. But when we transform it into healing for other people, something magical starts to happen. One, we start healing ourselves. The pain slowly goes away because you are acting out of compassion. You are doing what is right for the other person. There is a certain beauty to this. When we let go of those hurt feelings and turn our energy towards doing what is right for other people, we heal. And magically, we also start discovering the path to our purpose.

'The other thing that has worked for me is just having a sense of curiosity about a lot of things. *Oh, why is it like this? How does this work?* Awe, amazement, gratitude and not thinking about yourself and your feelings all the time works wonders. When you make space in your body and mind, you have a chance to listen to what others admire in you. All of us have amazing qualities, and many times, we may not be fully aware of them. Listening with mindfulness to what others admire in you will help you reflect.

'The other trick is to form a support group. Who are your cheerleaders among the people around you? Who will celebrate you every time you take a step closer to your purpose? Identify them and share with them. When you do these, you are formalizing the process of discovering your purpose. Something amazing starts to happen. Let me tell you a story.

> Once, there was an old, wise farmer. He was very respected because he would always give people sound advice. He had a son who was pretty useless. He would just sit around all day and while away his time. The old farmer knew that he would pass on at some point, and he was worried about what his son would do with his life.

Day 10: Purpose and Transformation

One day he called him and said, 'Look son, I want to tell you something. There is a secret treasure. If you find it, your life will be set. You won't have to do anything after that because when I pass, my wealth may not last you too long. Especially if you do nothing to add to it. But this treasure is so big that if you find it you don't have to do anything in your life. The son was very excited. He said, 'That's great, father. Show me how I can find this treasure.'

The old farmer packed the son's bag with clothes and some food. He gave him a map and said, 'Just follow this map and you will find it.'

The son set off after waving goodbye to his father. He travelled as fast as he could. In a few days, his food got over and the weather conditions became difficult. He was forced to stop. He was anxious because he was constantly thinking about the treasure. Once the weather improved, he started again. He rushed, travelling like that for six months because the map took him on and on.

Eventually, one day he reached the mountain where the 'X' was marked on the map. He located the exact tree. Under the tree, there was an 'X'. He started digging, but for a long time, he found nothing.

He was devastated that someone had stolen his treasure. He sat and cried for some time. Then he collected himself, saying, 'Okay. I might as well head back.' He started back and now the anxiety of finding the treasure was gone. So, he travelled much more peacefully. He stopped to admire the scenery. He spoke to people along the way and he ended up staying in some villages.

He learnt some new skills and became proficient at a few languages. He also began to practise some martial arts. Before he knew it, he had been travelling for two years. When he returned home, his father was fortunately still alive. He hugged his father and said, 'Father, I am so sorry; please forgive me for I didn't find the treasure.'

The farmer said, 'Son, why should I forgive you?' The son replied, 'You sent me out to find the treasure and I didn't find it, but you know what? I found so many other things.' He explained what all happened on his way back. He said, 'You know when I was going there, I was rushing. I didn't notice anything. I was falling and tripping over myself to reach there. When I finally did, there was nothing there. On the way back, I stopped and enjoyed everything a lot more. I have learnt so many more things.' The father then said, 'You know what, son? Let me tell you the truth. You have actually found the treasure I had hoped you would find.'

The son was amazed because he realized what his father had done for him. Though he had tricked him, he had also helped him discover so many things. In a sense, he had discovered his purpose. After that, the son really transformed. He started taking up responsibility around the farm. Eventually, the old farmer died and his son continued the tradition of giving people excellent advice.

'So, with that story, I want to leave you with the idea that discovering your purpose can be a beautiful process too. There is a little secret you can use as a guideline, because remember:

Day 10: Purpose and Transformation

Purpose is not a place.
Purpose is not a thing.
Purpose is a direction.

'Purpose is not set in stone. It can be something that shifts as everything else shifts around you, but the core remains the same. Create something to anchor yourself by—an object, a talisman. It could be a bracelet, a painting, a ring you wear or a tattoo. Find an object that reminds you of what your purpose is and have it in front of you. Keep it on your body, hang it on your wall—do whatever you want to with it, but keep reminding yourself of what that is. As you do that, you'll notice that some beautiful, amazing things start to happen to you. Maybe you will discover your purpose soon. Maybe it will take some time. But you will discover much more than the purpose itself as you go on that journey.

'All of us may not be a Michelangelo or Mozart, but doing whatever we do with a sense of purpose can make us a Michelangelo or Mozart at it. That, my friend, is how purpose works!'

Everything can have a purpose. If only we allow it!

Sid listened intently, the story of the farmer and his son settling deep within him. A thoughtful expression crossed his face as he sat quietly, letting the weight of Krish's words sink in.

'So it's the journey that matters, not just the destination,' Sid mused, a faint smile playing on his lips. 'The treasure isn't something out there—it's what you learn, what you become and what you discover along the way. It can be the same with purpose!'

He turned slightly, glancing up at the swaying branches of the mango tree overhead. The soft rustle of leaves seemed to mirror his own thoughts—gentle, yet persistent. Moving a little closer to Krish, Sid spoke with renewed curiosity.

'But here's the challenge, Krish,' Sid said, a hint of earnestness in his voice. 'In the midst of our busy day-to-day lives, we rarely notice these "signals", these lessons that could help us uncover our direction. Is there a way to catch them in a more structured or formal way? Something that we can actually plan for?'

Krish's smile widened, ready to guide Sid through the next layer of exploration.

'The simple answer to that question? Yes, there is a way. And the way includes all these practices. The way includes methods of stilling the mind. And as you do that, it improves your ability to read and interpret these signs. It is not that life is difficult and is not allowing us to achieve our purpose. We have made life difficult because we have completely lost control over the mind which tells you that life is like this or life is like that and this person or that situation is preventing you from achieving your purpose. Life is, in every single way, supportive of each one of us discovering our purpose. It is for us to open the gift wrapping and look inside. If we constantly keep saying, "Oh, right now it's too noisy, so I won't open; tomorrow it's too silent, so I won't open; day after, it is sunny, so I won't open; day after that, it is raining, so I won't open", then we are the ones who, ultimately, are responsible. So, how do we develop this capacity to unwrap this gift? It is through practising mindfulness and stilling the mind. Because at the end of the day, nobody else or nothing else prevents you from going on this journey. Everything and everybody else is there to support you. You just need to see it.'

Sid's fingers traced absent patterns as he processed Krish's words. His thoughts swirled, gradually settling into clarity. *Life isn't against me—it's waiting for me to see it clearly,* he reflected, a faint smile tugging at the corners of his mouth.

'That's all. I hope that didn't confuse you more!' Krish chuckled and said. 'It is a very nuanced aspect and this is what I'm trying to say:

Shift your perspective. See life, people and circumstances not as obstacles, but as challenges which are there to help you uncover and engage your purpose and superpowers.

Sid sat quietly, his gaze fixed on the ground as he let Krish's words sink in. After a moment, he straightened up and looked towards Krish with a thoughtful expression. 'I understand. If I bring awareness to shape my perspective, I can find that life supports my purpose. But I've been thinking . . . is the direction of the mind a natural corollary to rationality? I wonder—if I focus too much on being at peace and being satisfied with what I already have, will that suppress my passion to get things done?'

'This is a popular misconception. There is absolutely no contradiction. It's because peace is an internal state that comes out of great clarity and calm. The byproduct of that is not the lack of passion. In fact, a great intensity will bring passion towards the right things. If you find peace on the inside, you fix almost everything on the outside. That's when you have complete clarity about your passion. This seeming dichotomy is probably because either there isn't complete peace on the inside or what you are trying to go after is not synchronizing with that peace on the inside.'

Passion fizzles out when the purpose is not defined and articulated.

Sid nodded slowly, absorbing Krish's response. He stood and shifted his weight slightly, standing straighter now as if a weight had lifted off him. 'That makes sense,' he said thoughtfully. 'So peace isn't the enemy of passion—it's the foundation that makes passion clear and sustainable.' He paused, his curiosity deepening. 'But Krish, is it alright to review our purpose from time to time? And if it changes?'

'Of course!

Purpose is not a destination. It's a direction.

'It can change with your life phases and stages. What the purpose of life is at a certain point speaks to that stage or phase of life. Purpose has a meaning which is slightly larger than just oneself. So, when you think of it like that, you can have a short-term purpose and a long-term purpose. The short-term purpose could be to achieve financial security but your long-term purpose could be being of service to humanity.

'It's like when you are driving on the highway, you are looking further ahead and also at the road right in front of you. You keep toggling between the two and it is possible that these two change as the landscape changes. The universe wants you to be a co-creator in your destiny, and it is not handing you down fate on some piece of paper. You may identify your purpose, but if life has some different plans for you, instead of getting upset, go with the flow and discover a different purpose. That's how it works.'

Sid's gaze lingered on the horizon, the shifting colours of the sky mirroring the thoughts swirling inside. Krish's words felt like a gentle nudge, encouraging him to embrace the fluidity of purpose rather than fear its evolution. Krish's voice softened, breaking the reflective silence. Everything around them seemed to pause, as though the moment itself was inviting a breath.

Purpose, like life itself, evolves.
It's fluid—both a guide and something you co-create
as you go.

'Let's take a purposeful break now. A little time to reset and nourish ourselves,' laughed Krish as he stood and started to walk towards the cottage.

Sid nodded, absorbing Krish's words, and stood up, stretching briefly as he felt the heaviness of the morning's reflections lift slightly. 'You're right. A little break will be good.'

Sid decided that he would take a walk and practise mindfulness by observing nature around him. As he started focusing on becoming more present, he could feel his energies also shifting and greater clarity emerging.

Later, Sid made his way to the quiet dining area. A simple meal was waiting for him—a bowl of rice, lentils and fresh vegetables. Instead of mindlessly eating while scrolling on his phone as he used to in the past, Sid had started to practise mindfulness with his meal based on Krish's earlier teachings.

He sat at the small table, placing the plate in front of him. He paused, took a deep breath and allowed his gaze to soften as he observed the colours and textures of the food. The yellow of the lentils, the bright green of the sautéed vegetables, the warm steam rising gently from the rice.

Lifting his hands to the plate, he clasped them gently for a moment in gratitude. 'Thank you for this meal as well as the people and the hands that made it possible,' he whispered softly.

As he picked up the first bite, Sid slowed down even more. He noticed the weight of the spoon, the feel of the food as it touched his lips, and the subtle flavours—earthy, nutty, tangy—that revealed themselves as he chewed slowly. He could hear the faint rustle of leaves above him, the chirping of birds in the distance.

For the first time today, eating took on a different dimension. Sid felt deeply present, savouring each mouthful, noticing how it nourished his body and settled into his stomach with warmth. A wave of calm washed over him, and for a brief moment, everything felt enough.

By the time Sid finished his meal, his mind felt clearer, as though the act of eating mindfully had in itself become an anchor to the present. He sat quietly for a few minutes longer, letting the sense of fullness and gratitude linger before walking across to his room.

As the sun began its slow descent that evening, casting golden streaks across the sky, Sid found Krish seated under the open veranda, gazing thoughtfully at the horizon.

Krish turned as Sid approached, a knowing smile spreading across his face. 'Feeling recharged, Sid?'

'Yes,' Sid replied with a gentle nod. 'I again practised mindful eating today, and something shifted. It's so strange—I feel lighter, more connected to something . . . I can't quite put it into words.'

Krish's smile deepened. 'That's the magic of mindfulness—it starts to align your mind, body and actions. And when that kind of alignment happens . . .' He paused for effect, his tone shifting into the steady calm of a guide ready to lead the next exploration, 'you transform.'

Sid listened intently. Something told him that this was going to be a natural conclusion to what he had started ten days ago!

'And when you transform, you give up the old. We often have very fixed notions of who we are and these notions can actually prevent us from transforming. If you want to sail away from one port, you have to leave the shore behind. Similarly, if you keep holding on to who you are, how will you become who you might be?

Only when you let go of who you are now can you become who you might be.

'Transformation starts with slowly letting go of all these things that we have told ourselves, the stories that we've built around ourselves. Only when we start to leave behind all of that do we allow space for new things to grow. There's a wonderful story of a very famous Zen master.

Nan'in was widely loved and well-respected. He used to live in a simple cottage all by himself. People would come from near and far to listen to him. They would learn a lot and go back with deep respect for the man.

There was a professor of philosophy who was very upset with the monk because people loved him and respected him so much. So, one day, he decided to go and confront the Zen master. He went to his house and said, 'I am a professor of Zen philosophy and I have read all the scriptures. What do you know? Let me tell you what Zen is. Let me tell you what philosophy is,' and he just continued talking.

Nan'in was sitting at a table. Eventually, he picked up two cups and a kettle. He kept a cup in front of the professor and a cup in front of himself. He started pouring the tea from the kettle into the professor's cup. He kept pouring till the cup started overflowing. And he didn't stop. The professor finally shouted at him, saying, 'Hey, what are you doing? Can't you see that my cup is full? Why are you pouring more? It's overflowing.' So Nan'in said, 'You are exactly like that. You have come here to tell me how much you know about Zen and philosophy and everything else. Your cup is so full. Unless you empty it, how will you know what I know?'

'This simple and beautiful story of how we need to keep emptying our cup to be able to replenish it applies to all of us. So, when we talk of transformation, the first step starts with shedding the old.'

Sid stood up slowly, his hands slipping into his pockets as he gazed at the twilight sky where hues of orange were softening into purple. He turned back to Krish, his expression thoughtful, a small smile on his lips.

'That's a powerful story, Krish,' he said, his voice steady but reflective. 'I suppose we're all walking around with full cups, thinking we know who we are, what we're capable of and what we're supposed to do. But unless we let go of these ideas—shed the old stories we tell ourselves—there's no room for transformation.'

Sid paused, shifting his weight onto one foot, the realization settling deeper within him. 'It makes me think . . . maybe my own cup has been a little too full too.' Krish nodded, a glimmer of approval in his eyes.

'When we keep thinking that we are growing old, we grow old. But when we keep growing, there's no concept of becoming "old". It's a natural process. That's all there is to it. The shift in perspective is to think you are constantly growing. The physical body grows through youth and then it starts to stabilize. Mentally, emotionally and spiritually, though there is no plateauing out. You can continue to grow right through your life. And when you do that, it does some amazing things to even the physical aging process.

'There are more than thirty trillion cells in our body. Many of them die and new ones grow in their place. In three weeks' time, we grow a completely new layer of skin. It's like new clothes every three weeks.'

Sid listened intently, his thoughts turning over the idea of constant renewal. The notion of growth—physical, emotional and spiritual—felt both inspiring and grounding. He could almost feel the shift in his perspective, a quiet excitement stirring within him.

Krish smiled, as if sensing Sid's thoughts, and continued, 'Many cells in the body replace themselves within ten years. You can look at it this way—every ten years, you have a new body. Interestingly, brain cells live the longest. And they don't really get replaced. So what becomes even more important is that while the physical body has a built-in natural mechanism of transformation, the brain requires a little more conscious effort. Constantly bringing growth into this process is an amazing way of transformation through choice, not through autopilot or by default.

'Epigenetics shows that the life and health of our body cells is largely influenced by their environment. Which means that if you are responding with stress, you release certain chemicals into your body. And those chemicals form the environment of the cell to which it responds. You may consider yourself an individual, but a cellular biologist will say you are a cooperative community of approximately thirty trillion cells.'

As Krish spoke, Sid closed his eyes and let his imagination take over. He pictured himself in a smog-filled city, the air thick and heavy, stinging his lungs with every breath. The water he drank tasted metallic, tainted by pollutants. The streets were noisy, chaotic and overwhelming, leaving him tense and on edge. His body felt sluggish, weighed down by the toxic environment surrounding him. Krish's voice gently pulled him back.

'When the environment for your cells becomes stressful, they start to mutate. That is nothing but cancer. The environment is something that we create. The body consists of many physical elements. But a lot of these chemicals and hormones that are released into the body are a result of our responses and reactions. Therefore, we bring mindfulness into the picture. Because if we are mindful, each of those cells is going to say, "Wow, I live in a beautiful environment. This is like a holiday resort." The cell will automatically respond in positive ways with great health and well-being. If all cells are happy and in good health, you'll see it in the overall health of the body, right?

'Once you do this, the nature of these cells gets passed on in the DNA. So, if today we transform ourselves into beautiful, powerful human beings, we pass that on to the next generation. Nurture in turn impacts nature.'

Sid stood motionless, his gaze fixed on the distant horizon. Krish's words hung in the air, resonating deeply within him. The idea that transformation could begin at such a microscopic level—within the very environment of his cells—felt both profound and empowering.

He let out a slow breath, his voice soft but certain. 'So, it all begins with the environment I create for myself, both in my mind and body . . . that's where transformation truly starts.'

Krish tilted his head slightly, a thoughtful expression softening his features as his eyes met Sid's. His voice was calm, yet inviting, as if encouraging Sid to ponder the question deeply.

'Tomorrow morning, let's say you wake up without any memory of when you were born. You don't have a passport or any ID proof that tells you your birth date. You wake up and have forgotten how old you were. How old would you be? Just reflect on that silently. There is a chronological age, which is what our documents say. There is a biological age, which is how old our body is. There is a mental age, which is how old the brain and mind are. There is emotional age and spiritual age, too. Just reflect on how all these cater to you.

How old would you be if you didn't know how old you were?
What would you do if you didn't know you couldn't do it?
Why are you alive?
What would you be ready to die for?

'Would you just pick up an instrument and try to play it? Would you try to speak another language? Would you go paragliding? What if children grow up with a sense of adventure without the parent being there to say, "You can't do that!" or "Don't do it because you can't do it."? Imagine what could happen to a child?

'Within our bodies, there is so much transformation happening without us being aware of it. Now, if we were to become more aware of it, can we manage all those physical transformations better? The body has a specified way of growth and peaking. On the other hand, the mind can keep peaking forever. So, it is important for the old to give way to the new.

'Trees grow leaves which stay through the season, but eventually fall and give way to new leaves. Similarly, if we become aware of the process of transforming ourselves, we can dramatically change the way our life operates, both at a physical level and otherwise.

'Start looking at how well you have lived, how well you are living. Do not resist change and say, "No, this is who I am! I will cling on to it so tightly that I cannot transform", or "I'm too old to transform." Earlier, it was thought that our brains develop only for the first fifteen to twenty years of our lives and then stop. But now, science has shown that that is not true at any age. There are fascinating studies by acclaimed neuroscientists like Richard Davidson and Judson Brewer that have shown that practices of mindfulness alter certain parts of the brain. We can develop certain areas of our brain which can bring about positive changes in our lives. Additionally, we can even shrink other parts responsible for stress and fight-flight syndromes. Not just that, a number of these studies also show that with sustained practice, the altered states that these practices create, in fact become permanent traits!

'So, the question to ask is, how well have you lived? How well are you living?

In the end, we only regret the chances we didn't take. The relationships we were afraid to have and the decision we waited too long to make.

'How well do you want to shape your transformation going forward? Let's look at it through the lens of mindfulness and see how we can recognize and support some of these processes.'

'That's a powerful way to look at it,' Sid said thoughtfully, his voice calm but reflective. 'If I could forget my limitations—forget the labels of age, identity or what's holding me back—I wonder what I'd allow myself to try to become. I can see how much I've clung to the idea of who I am, thinking it's fixed. But maybe it's time to let some of those leaves fall, as you said . . . to make space for the new.'

He turned back to Krish, who stood a few paces away, his hands clasped gently behind him, watching Sid with a quiet smile. 'It's fascinating that transformation doesn't have to stop, no matter the age. The mind, the body—they can keep evolving. I think . . . I've been stuck clinging to the old, without realizing it.'

Krish nodded approvingly, stepping off the veranda into the garden with Sid following close behind. The setting shifted to a small clearing under the shade of a neem tree, where a light breeze swayed the leaves overhead. 'Come,' Krish said, gesturing for Sid to sit on a large flat stone. 'Let's do this practice out here—grounded, surrounded by nature.'

Sid lowered himself onto the stone, legs crossed and palms resting on his knees, while Krish settled onto a small patch of grass across from him. The dappled sunlight danced across their faces, and the soft hum of nature created an almost meditative soundtrack. Krish's posture was tall yet relaxed, as though he were effortlessly in sync with the earth beneath him.

'This space feels right,' Krish began softly, closing his eyes. 'Let's use this moment to connect to the idea of growth, of transformation. Just as nature does so effortlessly, so can we.'

Sid exhaled slowly, already sensing the quiet anticipation of what was to come.

'Find a way to sit that is both alert and relaxed. Notice your posture, your body. Take a few deep breaths. Breathe in, allowing the body to expand. Breathe out, allowing the body to relax. Let's give the body permission to relax so that we can observe the body and its transformation. Notice how the belly expands when you breathe in, how it contracts as you breathe out. Right now, there's nowhere else to be, nothing else to do. Just simply sit here, noticing your breath. Inhale and exhale deeply with the belly.

'Breathing normally, with no extra effort, notice the beginning of the inhalation. Notice how it goes in and how it ends. There is a gap at the end of the inhalation and the start of the exhalation. If the mind wanders, just gently bring it back.'

Sid's body settled into a rhythm of tension and release, each breath carrying him deeper into a sense of calm. He felt lighter, more attuned to his body, as though a quiet clarity was beginning to emerge. He waited, eyes gently closed, for Krish's next instructions.

'Now, take your attention to your feet and try to stretch their muscles as much as you can. Hold them this way. Then relax, letting go completely. Similarly, as you breathe in, try to clench your toes tightly. Hold them before you just relax the toes. See if you can do that with your lower legs. Just tighten the muscles in the lower legs and hold them. And then release.

'Take your awareness now to the upper legs, knees and thighs. Just clench and stretch the muscles as if you're lifting something. Hold it, then release it. Do this now with the abdominal muscles. Clench the muscles and hold them tight. Release.

'Do it now with the upper body, with the chest. Hold the breath and squeeze the lungs and the upper chest. And then release! Take your awareness into your fingers and make fists with your palms. Clench your fingers, squeeze them tightly and hold them that way. Hold, then release. Repeat that with your upper arms, biceps, triceps and shoulders. Release. And finally the neck, the head and the face. If you are able to, just clench your jaws a little bit and tightly squeeze your lips. You can even frown a little to tighten the facial muscles. Hold and then release. Now the whole body is relaxed—the whole body is limp.

'Now in your mind, imagine that your body is slowly changing and falling apart like dust and disappearing. Try to visualize this as intensely as possible. Now, take your awareness to your mind. If you visualize your body disappearing, your mind will already be calm. Silently observe your mind, letting go of all the thoughts. At this moment, everything is losing its relevance for you. There is no past, there is no future. When you start to imagine and visualize this, all thoughts will start disappearing from your mind. All thoughts exist only because you made them and there is no body, no mind and no thoughts.'

Sid felt the tension dissolve completely from his body, as if each muscle had surrendered to stillness. With Krish's words guiding him, he imagined his body breaking apart into tiny particles, like grains of sand scattering into the wind. Piece by piece, he visualized his form dissolving—feet, legs, hands, torso—until nothing remained but a vast emptiness.

In this state, his awareness turned inward, quiet and unshaken. The mind, usually restless, seemed to mirror the stillness of his body. The swirl of thoughts began to fade, one by one, like wisps of smoke vanishing into the air. Time lost its hold—there was no yesterday, no tomorrow—just a deep, expansive presence where even the boundaries of his own self seemed to dissolve. Sid floated in this space, weightless and serene, as though he were one with silence itself.

'Take your awareness now to the emotions that you might be experiencing by simply first becoming aware. Then remind yourself there is no body, no mind. There are no emotions as well. Just let them go. Let us now allow our whole body to mix with the universe.'

As Sid sat following Krish's gentle guidance, he felt an unexpected lightness. It was as if from the swirling chaos of thoughts a calm, unspoken clarity started to surface. Sid experienced a stillness that wasn't just an absence of noise but an invitation to something deeper. He noticed the subtle but profound shift. A sense of space appeared where the weight of his emotions once resided. In this stillness, he became curious: *What remains when I let everything else go?* As Krish's voice encouraged him to explore this space further, Sid allowed himself to step into this new and profound presence—the observer within.

'You will notice that something remains when the body, mind and emotions have gone. You can feel its presence. This observer is the real you. Just allow yourself to feel that presence. Now, imagine the whole body coming back from the universe. In your mind's eye, you can visualize particles flying through the universe and coming together to form your body. Slowly, the body starts to take its physical form. You can now take your awareness into the body and notice that the body is still here. Notice that your feet are touching the ground, the arms are touching the legs or each other. Notice the weight of the body on the chair. The body has now come back and it's a new body, reconstructed. Take your awareness now to your mind. How does the mind feel? Simply observe the quality of your mind now. Without any expectations or judgment, noticing if it is the same or different. Then take your awareness to the centre of your heart, the top of your chest. Notice if any emotions are becoming apparent to you. What kind of emotions are you experiencing now?

'You have gone through a small but powerful process of transformation. Now, bring to mind an intention that you have for yourself. What is this journey of transformation for you? Recall what you would like to transform into. Allow that to gently come into the light. Let go of all thoughts, taking your awareness back to the body. Make a small, gentle movement with your fingers and notice the sensations that arise. Gently move your toes. Notice the sensations again. With one deep inhalation and exhalation, whenever you are ready, gently and softly open your eyes. Allow the outer world to meet with the new inner world that you have created.'

As Sid followed Krish's words, he felt himself drifting into an even deeper state of stillness. His awareness turned to the subtle emotions lingering within him—hesitation, calm, perhaps even a quiet awe. But as Krish reminded him of the absence of body, mind and emotions, Sid felt a profound sense of release, as if he were gently untying knots that had been holding him for years. The emotions dissolved like mist under the morning sun, leaving behind an indescribable spaciousness.

Sid manifested a clear intention, an image of the person he wished to become—a leader guided by purpose and compassion, someone at peace with himself yet driven to make a difference. The vision settled gently within him, like a seed planted in fertile soil.

As he slowly moved his fingers and toes, Sid felt a tingling aliveness return. Opening his eyes softly, he met the golden light of the evening. The world around him was the same, yet everything looked different—sharper, brighter, alive.

He blinked slowly, a faint smile playing at his lips, feeling the deep transformation within him. Krish's voice broke the quiet moment, warm and calm as ever.

'Welcome to the new, transformed version of you. In a sense, you are reborn because you went through the process of allowing the body to disappear and go into the universe. You allowed the mind to go blank, all thoughts to fade away. You allowed all emotions to leave you. And finally, you noticed there was still something left behind. Then you reconstructed everything.

'On this journey of transformation, we have looked at so many aspects and perspectives. Now, it's about applying these learnings together. You must put all of this to use to live in the present moment. Because the present moment is all that there is. The past and future are only in our minds. It's about simply living every single moment well, with intention, intensity, passion, purpose, and self-awareness. You have to deal with your emotions, be kind, empathetic and compassionate. If you were to combine all of these, you will take a very powerful step towards being fully aware with every passing moment.

'Practise is the key. The solution to all human problems is individual inner transformation. If each one of us can completely transform and become the best version of ourselves, problems wouldn't exist. Let's not worry about the other people in our lives. Change begins with you. Change begins at home. And home is here. Home is not necessarily a space with bricks and steel. Home is inside. So, when you fix the inside, you fix the outside. And I truly believe that all of these processes can help you bring about that transformation.'

Sid sat quietly, letting Krish's words settle within him like seeds waiting to sprout. The simplicity and truth of it struck him—*change begins with you*. He took a deep breath, feeling a renewed clarity and resolve. Sid nodded thoughtfully, processing the insights. After a brief pause, he asked, 'How much time does one take to transform?'

'In the world today, everything is on demand. Movies, clothes, food, shopping. And in a world like this, you would expect transformation to also be on demand. Typically, transformation, by definition, means a rate of change that happens in a fairly short period of time. If a person has changed over a lifetime, I'm not too sure you can call it transformation. One person might take weeks and another person could take months.

'It depends on each one of us. It depends on the amount of effort that goes into it. For example, I was a practitioner of contemplative mental training practices for twenty-five years. Nothing happened as such. However, at one point, I made the flip. But underlying that was a lot of practise. So, transformation at the end of the day can be quick, but it also can be based on a long-term build-up of the qualities that underlie that transformation.

'Usually, people speak of physical transformation in terms of body-building and losing weight. But underneath it, there are some qualities such as determination which that person might have had for a long time. They just didn't put it to use.

'With mindfulness and meditation, you can keep at it. In the beginning, nothing may happen. But as you keep practising, you will see changes. A fleeting sense of something coming and going. And then, as you deepen your practice, something stays. You go from temporarily altering your state, to creating permanent traits!'

Sid's thoughts lingered on Krish's words, weaving them with his own experiences. He considered the moments in his life when change had felt within reach but seemed fleeting, as if he hadn't yet built the foundation for true transformation. The idea of effort layered over time resonated deeply with him. Sid's gaze drifted to the horizon, his eyes reflecting a quiet determination. He crossed his arms loosely, tapping his fingers gently against his elbow as he spoke. 'Krish, I've been thinking . . . how can I perform these deep practices on my own?'

'When you learnt a new language, sport or instrument—what happened? You worked with a teacher, right? Then as you got better and better at it, you started doing it on your own. As you deepen your practice, you will slowly be able to take off the training wheels. A day will come when you'll be able to go on your own a little bit. After a few minutes, you may get distracted. But as you deepen your practice, your capabilities and confidence will improve. You'll start to create a positive cycle.

'When I started in my early twenties, I couldn't sit in one place and meditate. I used to be restless with a hyperactive mind. I just couldn't do it. I almost gave it up saying, "Oh no, this is not for me." And then I discovered other aspects to it which helped me finally realize that meditation is not something you do. It's a state you are in. Use every moment as an opportunity to remain in that state. All those learnings will come and support you.'

Sid nodded slowly, letting Krish's words sink in. He thought about his own journey—how often he had dismissed practices like meditation as too difficult, not meant for someone with his restless energy. Yet now, sitting here, he could see the value in starting small, allowing things to unfold naturally over time. The idea of transformation as a process resonated with him. *If I can shift my own mindset and habits, what ripple effects could that have?* he wondered.

Sid's thoughts turned to his work and the challenges he faced leading his team. Looking up at Krish, Sid asked with curiosity, 'This process of transformation—how can business organizations be transformed with it?'

'What is an organization? It consists of organisms called people. And without people, there is no organization. If each of us can transform ourselves internally, automatically things on the outside will transform. If you inspire your team, department or unit to transform, at the end of the day, the whole organization will benefit from this transformation. By bringing mindfulness into the culture, creating rituals around it, training people and supporting them will transform the organization as a whole. The execution is obviously complex but it certainly can be done. The impact on improved productivity, creativity and innovation is also truly transformational.'

Sid tilted his head slightly, his brow furrowing as he processed Krish's words. He uncrossed his arms, a thoughtful expression taking hold. After a pause, he asked, 'In the corporate world, we talk so much about being agile and nimble. Does that mindset do justice to the transformation process? Or are we just struggling and striving to prove something?'

'You have to be agile and nimble. However, we also need to ensure that we are creating the right systems and processes to support that agility and nimbleness. You could move very quickly from one point to another without achieving anything, but that's not the point. Agility and nimble-footedness has to result in something positive. That's where something like mindfulness will help bring about a positive outcome, a transformation. Mere agility without transformation is of no use.'

Sid sat on his knees, running his fingers through the blades of grass beside him, as if grounding himself in the moment. 'That makes sense,' he murmured thoughtfully. After a brief pause, he looked back at Krish, curiosity sparking again. 'How do I construct my mindfulness practice to become a powerful one?'

'Regularity and sustainability are key. You have to keep practising to make it really effective and to get to a good place. This can take time, depending on how much effort you put into it. I have seen that some people practise every day and bring about results in a few months. Others are a little more gradual and they take maybe a few years. So, construct something for yourself that is healthy, sustainable and realistic. Waking up very early to practice mindfulness may not be sustainable for too long. You may do it for a couple of days and then stop. Construct something that is not too harsh on you and integrates mindfulness into a way of life.'

Sid smiled faintly, his gaze drifting towards the gentle sway of nearby trees, their leaves catching the late evening light. He shifted his posture, sitting up straighter as if readying himself for the next insight. 'That makes sense,' he said, his voice steady. 'Sustainability is key. And I think the insight of integrated practices can really help me do that. After a brief pause, he looked at Krish with renewed curiosity. 'So, if you had to narrow it down—what are the top two or three ingredients that are truly important for transformation? What should one keep in mind?'

'You already know the ingredients! The first, and the most important, ingredient is intention. You should want to transform. It's not for somebody else to transform you. The need should come from within. As desperate for air as you would get if held underwater for a long time.

'The next thing is the process of transformation itself. It has to be thought through. It has to be constructed mindfully with adequate help from other people. What is your support system like? Who is your transformation coach? Who are your cheerleaders? You need that motivation. Who all are giving you feedback and telling you how your transformation is going?'

Intention, intensity and right action—these I would say are the top three ingredients for transformation.

As Krish finished speaking, his voice softening with the weight of his final words, a serene stillness settled between them. The sun had dipped low into the horizon, bathing the sky in hues of deep orange and soft pink. A gentle breeze rustled the trees, carrying with it the faint, sweet scent of blooming flowers.

Sid remained quiet for a few moments, letting Krish's words wash over him. *Intention, intensity, action.* The simplicity of it struck a chord, yet the depth lingered like ripples on water. He glanced at Krish who sat with his hands resting lightly on his knees, his gaze fixed on the glowing horizon as if watching time itself slow down.

Sid stretched his legs out, grounding himself in the cool earth beneath the wooden bench they had shared for the last hour. 'Intention, intensity and right action,' he repeated softly to himself, as though trying to etch them into his mind forever.

The evening sounds began to awaken around them. The rhythmic chirp of crickets mixed with the distant hum of cicadas, creating a calming melody of nature's evening song. The golden sunlight filtering through the trees turned dusky, making way for a deeper, quieter light.

Krish finally broke the silence, his voice carrying a smile. 'It's been a long day, hasn't it?'

Sid nodded, a small smile tugging at his lips. 'Yeah . . . it's been a long day, but one I won't forget.' He ran his fingers through his hair, feeling a satisfying mix of exhaustion and contentment. 'You've given me so much to think about. I don't even know where to start.'

Krish chuckled lightly. 'Start where you are. Tomorrow will take care of itself.'

Sid stood, stretching his back and arms, and exhaled deeply, as though releasing the weight of all his reflections. He turned towards the horizon, where the last glimmers of daylight were melting into twilight. 'I think I'll take a walk,' he said quietly. 'Maybe sit around for a while.'

Krish nodded in approval, his expression calm and understanding. 'Good idea. Sometimes the best way to process things is to simply let them settle. Go be with yourself. Home is inside you.'

'The way out is in.'—Thich Nhat Hanh

Sid smiled gratefully, slipping his hands into his pockets as he began to walk away. The gravel crunched softly under his feet as he moved along the winding path. Shadows lengthened around him and the world seemed to exhale into a peaceful night.

As he walked around, Krish's words echoed softly in his mind—*Intention. Intensity. Right action.* A deep resolve began to form within him, like the first spark of a flame. Tonight, beneath the stars and the quiet companionship of the breeze, he realized this was just the beginning of something far greater.

He took a deep breath and began to make his way back to the cottage. There was a peacefulness in the air that he hadn't felt in a long time—a quiet clarity that seemed to come from deep within.

Back inside his room, Sid lit the small lamp and its warm glow filled the room. He sat down at the small wooden desk by the window where the soft breeze filtered in after having passed through the bamboo shoots outside. He pulled out his journal, the pages already filled with reflections and realizations from the past days. Sid opened to a fresh page, the tip of his pen hovering over the paper for a moment before he began to write.

Day 10: Purpose and Transformation

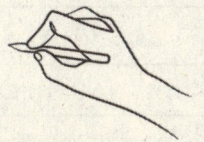

Tonight feels different. There's a stillness within me that I haven't felt in years.

Krish's words about intention, intensity and right action keep echoing in my mind. They are simple yet profound.

Purpose isn't about arriving at a fixed place.

It's clear now that transformation isn't just about changing what's on the outside—it's about cultivating what's on the inside.

When you transform internally, the external world follows.

My intention moving forward: To live with mindfulness and purpose, to embrace every moment as an opportunity to grow and to approach transformation with both intensity and patience.

There's a part of me that feels ready now—ready to step into the next chapter, to bring what I've learned into my work, my relationships and my life.

Tonight, I'll sleep with a deep sense of gratitude—for Krish, for this place, for the conversations and for the quiet realization that everything I need is already within me.

Some roads you need to take alone. No friends, no family, no partner. Just you and the universe.

Reflection questions:

What are a few things I could explore as my purpose?

What areas of life am I holding back living?

What fears keep me from living my best life?

Who am I and who do I want to be? What am I prepared to do, let go of or change to achieve that?

My talisman . . .

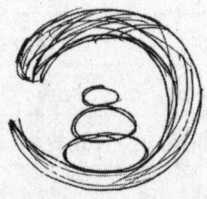

Sid sketched the circle of life. Strong and perfect in some parts. Frayed and broken in others. A symbol that life is a constant loop with no beginning or end, where one death gives rise to a new life. One that represents the infinite nature of energy. He saw himself sitting at the centre of this circle, trying to understand the paradox of life. Succeeding at times. Failing spectacularly at other times. This would become his guiding symbol. A tattoo that would serve as his lighthouse.

He closed the journal gently, running his hand over its cover. The room was quiet, the lamp's glow steady, as if mirroring his newfound calm. He blew out the flame, allowing darkness to settle into the room. Climbing into bed, he lay back with a contented sigh, the sound of crickets outside lulling him into a peaceful sleep.

For the first time, Sid felt ready—ready for whatever lay ahead.

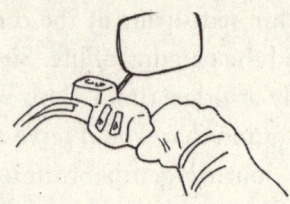

Day 11: Another Journey Begins

Sid woke up with a strange sense of excitement.

The soft hues of the early morning spilled gently over the farm as the sun peeked over the horizon, spreading warmth across the endless green fields. The air was fresh, carrying with it the earthy scent of damp soil mingled with the faint fragrance of blooming wildflowers. A cool breeze drifted in through Sid's open window, brushing against his face like a soft, reassuring touch.

Outside, the world was already alive. The rustling of the bamboo leaves created a calming rhythm, like whispers of farewell from the trees. Birds sang their morning melodies—chirps, tweets and calls that wove into a harmonious symphony. From somewhere near the lotus pond, a kingfisher let out its sharp cry, slicing through the stillness and calling attention to the beauty of the morning.

Day 11: Another Journey Begins

The distant low hum of insects preparing for the day buzzed faintly in the background. Somewhere in the distance, a cow let out a long, contented moo, as though it was also acknowledging the peace of the morning.

Sid took a deep breath as he stood by the window, inhaling the cool air and letting the calmness of the moment wash over him. The bamboo tree stood tall and strong, its leaves shimmering faintly in the early light. For days, he had looked at this tree, observing its stillness and strength. Today, it looked different—its resilience and grace seemed to reflect the new strength he felt within himself.

As he went about his recently created morning rituals, the excitement became more grounded and was replaced with a sense of great calm and clarity.

The last ten days with Krish had been nothing short of transformational. He felt like he had just completed a course which had covered everything that was skipped in business school. Everything that was paradoxically required for conscious leadership in the 21st century!

It was time to take his learnings and put them into action.

Intention + Intensity + Right Action—he recalled the powerful life lesson Krish had so elegantly taught him. The intention to transform his life and that of others around him was definitely there. He felt a certain kind of intensity—from the early sparks of ten days ago to now, it had become nothing short of a raging fire. It was clearly time for action.

Maybe I should speak with Krish today and seek his advice. Sid thought to himself. *I want to immediately start living all these lessons in my everyday life and leadership!*

Krish's cottage was unusually quiet. It almost felt deserted. As he looked around, he noticed a note on the table. Going up to it, Sid saw that it was for him.

Sid, a message came for me last evening. I have to go meet a friend. I'll be gone awhile.
Go to the lotus pond this morning.

Love,
K

P.S. There is someone I would like you to meet someday. Let me know when you are ready.

For a moment, Sid just stood there, the note in his hand. He read it again, as though trying to make sense of it. *Krish was gone?* A faint pang of disappointment touched his heart.

But then something about the message tugged at him. *Go to the lotus pond.* He tucked the note into his pocket, grabbed his shoes and stepped outside into the morning light.

The walk to the pond felt unnaturally quiet. Even the surroundings which were usually bustling with life seemed to share in the stillness. The lotus pond came into view like a scene from a dream. The water was perfectly tranquil, reflecting the sky as though it were a giant mirror.

There, in the centre of it all, the lotus flower stood. Fully open, its delicate petals spread wide as if embracing the morning sun.

Sid stood at the edge of the pond, his breath catching in his chest. For days, he had seen this flower, partly closed and growing inside, its beauty hidden from view. Now, it was in full bloom—a perfect, radiant pink, its petals touched with gold from the sunlight. It was breathtaking.

At that moment, Sid realized it was more than just a flower. It was a metaphor.

He understood why Krish had asked him to go to the lotus pond. The lotus had bloomed when it was ready—no sooner, no later. It had emerged through murky waters, unhurried and unforced, simply following its natural path.

It's time to bloom!, a voice whispered in Sid's head.

The realization filled him with a calm acceptance. Krish had prepared him for this moment all along. There were no more lessons, no more words needed. The journey here had led him to this point and now it was his turn to take what he had learned and carry it forward.

Sid knelt by the water's edge, taking in the sight of the lotus one last time. Its reflection shimmered softly on the surface, a reminder of what transformation could look like—graceful, patient and inevitable.

As his gaze lingered, he noticed his own reflection in the water. For the first time, he looked deeply into himself—not just the face staring back, but the quiet confidence, the calm in his eyes. He smiled softly, a knowing smile, as if acknowledging the profound changes that had taken root inside of him. The man reflected in the water wasn't the same person who had arrived here ten days ago. He had shed something old and something new had begun to bloom.

The walk back to the cottage felt different. Each step was lighter, but there was a quiet resolve behind it. When he entered, the space felt emptier without Krish, yet fuller with meaning.

Sid finished throwing his stuff into his saddlebags. He wanted to say so much to Krish but didn't know where to even begin.

Maybe I'll leave him a note for now, he thought to himself. *I can always come by and see him again.*

He entered Krish's room hesitantly. He had seen a little table by Krish's window and it seemed like a note left there would not get lost or misplaced till he returned.

That's when his eyes fell on a picture on the table. It was a photo of Obama shaking hands with a man in a business suit. As Sid looked at it closely, it struck him like a bolt of lightning.

That was none other than Krish! In the picture he looked very different—cropped hair, groomed beard and a crisp, tailored business suit. It was Krishna Kumar, or KK as he was popularly known, the legendary ex-CEO of the world's biggest technology company. With a longer beard and with his now silver hair, Sid had completely missed recognizing him.

Krish had created waves in the corporate world with his leadership style and people had revered him for his wisdom. It had felt almost poetic when he had announced his retirement at an early age, saying that he wanted to pursue other dreams.

Everything made even more sense now. The leadership wisdom, the practical examples, the stories and techniques! It was all coming from his expertise and personal experiences.

Feeling lost for words, Sid tore out a page from his journal and picked up a pen from the table. *What can I even say to this man that would make sense?!* Sid wondered.

He took a few deep breaths and paused.

Thank you. It's been an honour, KK sir!
Eternal love and gratitude,
　Sid

Sid tightened the straps of his saddlebags around the Harley. The motorbike was gleaming almost as though it was also reborn and ready to roar.

His eyes fell on the well-polished Screaming Eagle exhausts that glinted like mirrors. Unlike the morning he had started this journey, calm, clear eyes looked back at him.

Sidharth smiled. The Buddha smiled back.

Acknowledgements

This book would not have been possible without a lot of people.

The thousands of participants across the world that I have been privileged to teach over many years and who have, in turn, taught me so much.

The mindfulness-based emotional intelligence and leadership training programmes I teach, including the Google-born Search Inside Yourself programme, for allowing me to meet, share and learn from so many incredible leaders.

My parents for being everlasting writing inspirations.

Revathi and Kumar for reviewing the early manuscript and their invaluable feedback.

Supriya for all the freedom without which I could not be who I have become.

Anamika, my friend, ideator, collaborator and conspirator.

Kalyani for the belief and encouragement, the illustrations and design ideas.

Sri for always becoming whatever I ask of him.

The team at Llama for helping me take these teachings to the world.

Roshni for all the editorial help and suggestions.

Radhika, Sakshi and the publishing team at Penguin.

And finally, all those who have been my cheerleaders over the years, too many to name here but you know who you are—thank you!

Scan QR code to access the
Penguin Random House India website